Soil and Soul:

Ministry and Faith in Rural Illinois

By Ray Warfel Jr.

Published by
Spiritbuilding Publishers
9700 Ferry Road, Waynesville, Ohio 45068

SOIL AND SOUL:
Ministry and Faith in Rural Illinois
By Ray Warfel Jr.

ISBN: 978–1955285–98–8

Layout by Katrina Warfel

Cover Photo by Kristy Perry

Spiritbuilding
PUBLISHERS

spiritbuilding.com

Mom's Senior Picture

Dad's Senior Picture

Dedication

For Mom and Dad

My parents always had a garden. I asked my mom once why she and dad gardened so much. (I'm sure dad has a little patch again this year.) As a child, I remember it being row after row of vegetables. "Your dad and I both grew up farming," she answered. "I guess it's just our way of staying connected to the soil." Aside from corn and beans, tomatoes and potatoes, mom and dad raised a bunch of kids - five of their own and many more that mom babysat. They all grew up to bless her. (Pr 31:28).

I'm middle aged now, likely the same age she was when she answered my question. I, too, grow a garden but even more, like my mom and dad, my soul is rooted in this same black soil and in the God they both love so much.

Forward

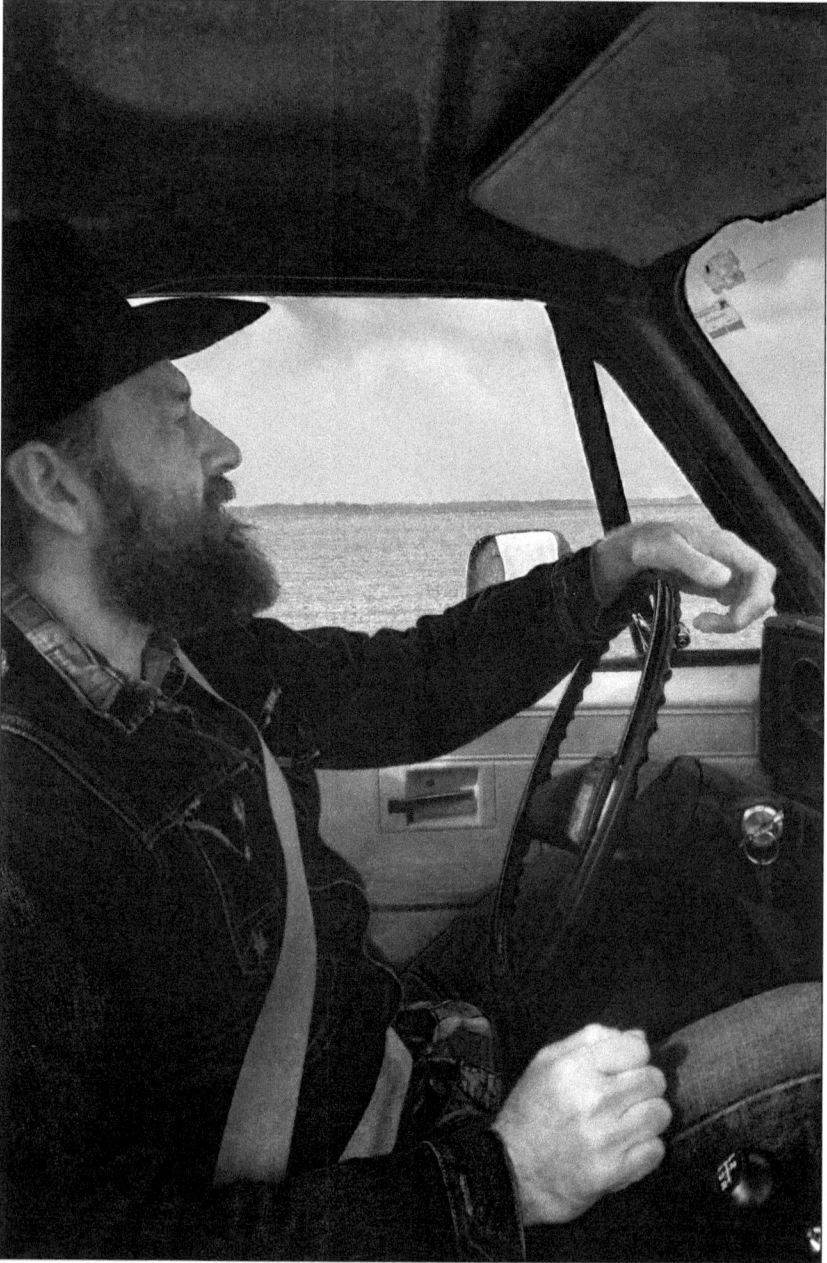

PHOTO TAKEN BY MY DAUGHTER MOLLY

My dad is the minister for a small church in rural Illinois. Pa doesn't consider himself a "pastor" but always refers to himself as a minister. All Christians are ministers, he just does it in a special way, and he says about preachers, "they can get preachy."

Unlike most ministers, my pa did not go to seminary, he did not have formal training. He doesn't even have a college degree, but he is just like the disciples. Jesus called just regular men with ordinary jobs. They didn't have a college degree, or training. As my dad says, "You don't have to have a degree, you just have to know the truth, love

God, and spend time with the Bible."

Pa serves a small church, just like the church of Philadelphia that Jesus wrote to (Rev 3:8). It was small and couldn't do a lot, it faced a lot of obstacles too. They only had a "little power" so what could they do for the Kingdom of God? "Jesus doesn't say one bad thing about them. They were a good and faithful church." Pa went on to say, "just because you're small doesn't mean you're doing it wrong, and just because you're big, doesn't mean you're doing it right." He also says, "Whatever we do as a small church or individually, we want to point people to God."

He's just a small-town preacher in rural Illinois, he is not advertising himself or highlighting a denomination. He is just pointing people to God. "If they don't know who I am, it doesn't matter. I want them to know who Jesus is."

I'm sure my pa will continue to preach until his last breath. He has joked with me saying that when he is old and can't get up on the pulpit anymore, he'll keep preaching from the pew or his wheelchair. Pa is just trying to point others to God. Even if it is just for a small-town church of only a few people. Pa says, "The small churches need preachers just as much as the big ones. If this is where God wants me, this is where I'll stay."

MEGAN WARFEL, APRIL 23, 2023
EDITED FROM A COLLEGE PAPER

Replanting the church

A SELECTION FROM A LETTER SEEKING SUPPORT FOR THE WORK

My grandfather's grandfather cultivated fields here in southern Illinois. He raised corn and wheat. My people raised families and they planted churches here. I have a cousin who still raises corn and wheat on our grandpa's place. He raises his family there too. But the church where my great-great grandfathers served as elders - where my grandpa was baptized, my dad grew up, and where I also once preached regularly in my youth - is gone. That church was not unique. There are so many like it in these small rural towns, dying when I was young and now, they have disappeared. Should these fields be abandoned like the dust bowl? Will another minister come here and love these people, my own people, more than me? Christians have tinkered in the machinery shed too long. We've busied ourselves maintaining the building and keeping the doors open, while the crops withered and the weeds overtook the field. Brethren, we are planting a church here. We are replanting these fields. Pray for us.

Mankind is My Business

What follows is a short selection from Charles Dickens' A Christmas Carol. The scene described is the night before Christmas where Scrooge is sitting alone in his chamber and the spirit of his old business partner, Marley, appears.

"Oh, captive, bound, and double-ironed," cried the phantom, "not to know, that ages of incessant labour by immortal creatures for this earth must pass into eternity before the good of which it is susceptible is all developed. Not to know that any Christian spirit working kindly in its little sphere, whatever it may be, will find its mortal life too short for its vast means of usefulness. Not to know that no space of regret can make amends for one life's opportunities misused! Yet such was I! Oh! Such was I!"

"But you were always a good man of business, Jacob," faltered Scrooge, who now began to apply this to himself.

"Business!" cried the Ghost, wringing its hands again. "Mankind was my business. The common welfare was my business; charity, mercy, forbearance, and benevolence, were all, my business. The dealings of my trade were but a drop of water in the comprehensive ocean of my business!"

Did you get that? It's written so well. Don't miss it.

"The dealings of my trade were but a drop of water in the comprehensive ocean of my business!" - Charles Dickenson

Life is about people. You appreciate that as you get older, and your circle of friends begins growing smaller. Death takes some. Hurt feelings and pride take others. Sometimes they vanish from thoughtless neglect.

When I was a boy, we'd have family dinner on Christmas Eve at my Grandpa Brooks' house. Aunts and uncles, cousins, everyone would come to fill the old farmhouse. The vintage aluminum Christmas tree was there (as always) and underneath were presents wrapped with new paper and topped with last year's bows (it was a thing - we always had to save the bows.) Supper time came and I'd scarf down beef noodles and a pile of mashed potatoes, both staples at Grandma's house. As soon as my plate was clean, I'd ask my dad if it was time for presents yet. "No, not yet. The grownups are still eating." Now, I knew better than to give my dad any back talk, but it looked to me like the grownups did a whole lot of talking. I figured that if they did more eating and less yakking, they'd be finished too. It's a matter of priority, after all, and to a six-year-old, Christmas was about presents.

That's a funny memory for me. Seriously though, I'd trade every present Grandpa ever gave me as a boy: the sleeping bag, the toolbox, even the pocketknife (the one still in my jeans pocket today.) Yes, I'd trade every one of those things for one more Christmas dinner with Grandpa. We'd eat beef noodles and potatoes. I might even try that oyster dressing he loved so much, but we'd talk most of all.

Mankind is my business. Keep the stuff... just give me the people. We all understand the truth of it even if we aren't very good at living it out in the day to day.

This is a simple prayer I offer to God rather often, like Tiny Tim's final benediction.

"God, I don't care so much what I have in life, where I go, or how high I climb. I don't care what chore you give me or what challenges lay ahead of me. God, I don't care anymore, just please God, let me be and enjoy pleasant and peaceable company along the way. Amen."

My Beloved Children

I suppose if I only had one sermon to share, it would be this one. It's one I share at just about every opportunity. The message is a look at the way the elderly apostle John addresses the readers of his first epistle. Sometimes he calls them "beloved" and other times "my little children." He alternates I think for the sake of variety but what I hear constantly are the words a good father says to his children. It's what our heavenly Father says to us and what I want my children to remember me saying to them. Here is a brief synopsis.

Good fathers say - Be careful. Look both ways before you cross the street. Don't talk to strangers (and many other words of caution.) The apostle John had spiritual dangers in mind too when he said, "Little children, make sure no one deceives you," and "Beloved, do not believe every spirit" and "guard yourselves from idols"(1 Jn 3:7; 4:1; 5:21).

Good fathers say - Remember who you are. Here's a little story to show this. "Where'd you get those big ears?" A little boy had been teased by a classmate. Upset, he told his dad about it when he got home that evening. His dad looked at him and said, "You just tell them your dad gave you those ears." I tell my children, "You may be a weirdo, but you're my weirdo." Apostle John said it like this, "Beloved, now we are children of God" (1 John 3:2). It doesn't matter what anyone else thinks about you, says about you, or how they judge you. If you are God's, He is proud of you and nothing anyone else says about it will change that fact.

Good fathers say - Be nice to your brothers and sisters. Siblings squabble. It's normal. I'm amazed that my siblings even talk to today when I think of my ornery childhood behavior. But we're all grownups and they love me despite that past childishness. I am at the same time ashamed of myself and humbled by their love because a day may come when your life crumbles and the only safe place you have left to crash is your sister's sofa. Be thankful for their love. They love you but don't make it a chore for them (1 Jn 3:18; 4:7, 11).

Good fathers say - Remember what I told you. It often comes in moments of frustration. Your child has been careless or misbehaving and you open your mouth, but it's your dad's words that spill out. Right then you realize - you have become your dad. John described this embodiment saying, "Beloved, I am not writing a new commandment to you, but an old... which you have heard. On the other hand, I am writing a new commandment to you, which is true in Him and in you" (1 Jn 2:7, 8). The faith is old, but it is renewed with every new believer. My father taught me the faith, but I don't have his faith. It's mine now.

Good fathers say - It's okay, I can take care of it. Dads fix bike tires and broken toys. We're fixers; it's what we do. How hard it is then, whether by sickness, a broken heart, or sin, we look at our broken child and know we cannot fix this. No, I can't fix it, but I know the Father who can (1 Jn 2:1).

Good fathers say - I love you (and they say it often.) Beloved. Beloved. Beloved. Six times John says this (1 Jn 2:7; 3:2, 21; 4:1, 7, 11). I don't understand why some people are so sparing and stingy with these words. Do you suppose they will lose their value the more we use them? I promise, they will not. Insincerity is the only thing to strip them of meaning. I don't want my children to ever wonder how I feel about them, so every time they visit or call or text me I tell them "I love you." And listen, your Father loves you.

Holding Hands

I held her hand today. We stood before our God, bowed in prayer, and I held her hand one last time. It's not as small as it was when she first gripped my finger as a baby, but it's still so soft and little wrapped in mine. We left the church building and drove past the house where I packed my silver Ranger in the summer of '96, where my mom hugged me and told me I could always come home. I hugged my daughter today... tight. Just like mom hugged me. I spoke the same words to her, the ones my mom spoke to me, the same ones I told her sister before.

"You'll always have a safe place here with your pa, a place to sleep, a seat at my table. If you're ever in trouble, no matter how mad you think I'll be, no matter how far apart we live, or how long it's been since we spoke last, I'll be here for you. I'd love to hold your and your sister's hands again. You can climb up in my lap and let me rock you; let me keep you safe. I'm proud of you. I'm pleased for you. Visit when you can. I'll check the oil and tire pressure. I'll fix you supper and mend the holes in your jeans. I'll hold your hand and I'll thank God for the years I had you at home. I love you."

I waved until I couldn't see her anymore and I waved a little longer too. Don't worry about me, like a good dad, my face was all steel as she drove off.

—

There is a special intimacy in holding hands, the gentle touch of another. "There was a man covered with leprosy, and when he saw Jesus, he fell on his face and implored Him, saying, 'Lord, if you are willing, You can make me clean.' And He stretched out His hand and touched him..." (Luke 5:12-13). Lonely, avoided, ignored this man may not have felt his children's hugs for years. How long had it been since his wife lay her fingertips softly on the back of his neck? Can he remember the last time a friend put an arm on his shoulder? It was such a small gesture but there was power in the touch of Jesus' hands. Not the healing of disease, but the acceptance, the comfort, and welcome.

I have a memory, as many country boys do, of riding on the fender of grandpa's tractor or sitting at his feet in the harvester. Those were special times, but I have a more powerful memory. I was a young father visiting my folks. My grandparents stopped by. As our visit ended, grandpa stood up next to me. We watched my girls give hugs and get their coats on. He took my hand in his. We didn't speak. He didn't even look at me. It was a small thing, holding hands, but it communicated everything that could not be said in an entire evening.

Last Sunday as our worship service was ending, I stood next to my daughter.

While we bowed to pray, I reached down and took hold of her hand. I don't know what it communicated to her, but when she squeezed my hand in return, I think she heard me. I make my living with words. I give my children counsel and advice and warnings. They have joked that I do most of my preaching Monday through Friday. But I know the power in just one touch.

Unconditional Love

"Faithful are the wounds of a friend, but deceitful are the kisses of an enemy" (Pr 27:6).

Nobody likes to be told they're wrong. I certainly don't enjoy it. But we need people in our lives who care enough for us to tell us the truth, especially truth that hurts to hear. For instance, I have a great coach at my local gym. The other day we were doing dead lifts. He can press significantly more weight than I can even though we are roughly the same size. Also, he has multiple years more experience in weight training than I have. When I step up to the barbell and reach down to grab hold of it, he starts pointing out all kinds of problems, from my head to my feet. He says, "get your hips back, Ray...Keep your heels down. Head up...Don't drop your shoulders... Brace your midline. Don't pull. Push the ground away." Sometimes when I'm tired, exhausted, and sweaty from the rest of our workout, I don't even want to hear his voice much less all his corrections. But he is my friend. He's looking out for my safety so that I don't seriously injure myself. People can and have hurt themselves. Wouldn't I have to be an arrogant fool to ignore him?

Now I wouldn't just accept anyone's input; opinions, after all, are like noses - everybody has one, some are just bigger than others. Like my gym buddy, however, there are people I respect, sometimes because of their age or experience or maybe the wisdom they have displayed in their own lives. These people's criticisms and cautions I'm glad to hear. Sometimes what they have told me has stung. It's not been what I've wanted to hear, but it's what I've needed to be told.

For my part, I too have told people things they did not want to hear, things about which they disagree with me. Maybe they feel that I don't love them because I refuse to encourage them on the destructive life path they are choosing. I don't say the things I do because I am mad at them or angry. Oh, it's the very opposite! I love them so very much. And true love, genuine love, real unconditional love wants more than anything else what is best for them.

I am confident that God the Father's commandments are not intended to be a burden or to spoil our fun (1 Jn 5:3). No, He instructs us and warns us for our good (Deut. 10:13). As a father myself, what I tell my children they should do and what I warn them against doing is not meant to make their life hard. Again, it's the opposite. I love them. I unconditionally love them and so I want to save them from needless hardships in their life.

I'll add one more comment. While God is always right, I know that I am not. I could be wrong in my opinions or how I understand the Bible. And so, if someone really loved me, they would tell me, show me, or help me see where I'm wrong. They wouldn't just walk away and cut me off.

Men Leave a Mark

An old china cabinet used to sit in an even older farmhouse in Stamping Ground, Kentucky. The wear on this cabinet's varnish was interesting. On one corner it was completely gone, worn down to bare wood. The old man would sit in the kitchen when he came in from working, resting his arm on the cabinet's shelf until he rubbed away the varnish. After many years, he left a mark.

Often when we see an abuse, we run to the opposite extreme assuming this other side must be better by default. We want to move as far from one wrong as we can, but by overcorrecting, we miss one ditch only to crash into the other. Some men are domineering and cruel. Some are self-serving. They leave scars and pain and damaged souls behind them. I have heard these men and these behaviors condemned in church and culture alike from the time I was a small boy.

Some of us (I do not think I am entirely unique) are softer and gentler by nature. We hear of those wrongs and want to avoid them. We hear the Scriptures that call us to be gentle, peaceable, loving, compassionate, and kind. We want to be that. It's easy for us. Easy to be soft spoken. To live and let live. To have a soft touch and a light step. I don't think I could be domineering if I tried, but we gentle men are imbalanced too. We're like a weight lifter who always skips leg day. Please understand - being decisive is not arrogant. Having vision is not toxic. Leading is not abuse. These traits are masculine, and more importantly, they're godly. Some men need to cultivate a softer hand. They ought to read and embody verses like: Gal 5:23; Eph 4:2; Phil 4:5; Col 3:12; 1 Tim 6:11. Others of us need to embrace a stronger confidence.

Godly men leave a good mark on the world. In the Old Testament, God chose Abraham, "so that he may command his children and his household after him" (Gen 18:19). Abraham not only had a right but a God given responsibility to be decisive, to point people in a direction and then move them toward it.

Godly men speak up. In his old age Joshua said, "as for me and my house, we will serve the Lord" (Jos 24:15).Years before he said this, he, along with Caleb, had opposed the cowardice of all the men of Israel.

Godly men stand for what is right...not just in their hearts and not just at home in private (though they do need to make a stand at home.) They don't only take a stand with like-minded people at church. Wherever a man is he ought to "build up the wall and stand in the gap before Me for the land" (Eze 22:30).

There will be those who will want men like this in theory, but not in practice. Most of the culture won't want them either way. Let the Jezebels call you toxic. Let their harem of weak-willed Ahabs call you the problem, the troubler of our time. Let them all rage. Make your mark in this world because godly men answer to God.

The More People I Talk with, the More I Like People

Today I visited with a friend at a long-term care facility. He was busy when I arrived. While waiting in the large visiting room, another patient was wheeled in near where I was sitting. We began talking. She told me it was her ninetieth birthday this month. She'd been married sixty-three years before her husband passed away. Together, they lived here and there around the country.

She talked about her childhood. Her grandmother sent her out into the yard to collect some kind of grass to bake into what she called grass pie. She didn't remember what kind of grass it was. Someone overheard us. They shouted across the room that they used to make mud pies, but no one would eat that. We all laughed. The woman I'd been speaking with replied that she liked to make mud pies when she was a girl and once even talked a boy into taking a bite. "I guess he must have liked me," she said. Again, we all laughed.

She talked about her dad a lot. She said he made her go to church every Sunday. She would ride with a friend to Catholic mass and then go to the Christian church on her own. She told me her dad insisted she go but would tell her, "Those church people do some good things but don't listen too much to what they say." A person just never knows who they will meet in a day.

Not a Business-Like Prayer

The main article in this week's bulletin is very personal to me. At a gospel meeting this week, I was asked to dismiss the assembly in prayer. What follows is roughly what I quickly sketched out on my notebook before the end of the sermon which was entitled "The Wife Your Husband Needs." This was deeply personal to me because I had to divorce my wife of sixteen years. Coincidentally, the man preaching that night and the night before on the subject, "The Husband Your Wife Needs", was the same man who performed our wedding ceremony.

After praying, I got a bit emotional. I couldn't seem to help it. I'm embarrassed that I can't speak sincerely without my voice quivering a little. After the "Amen", my son came up and told me he had heard prayers like that before. He said, "It sounded like a Tony prayer." Tony is my youngest brother. I asked what he meant; what is a "Tony prayer?" His response will likely be the most treasured compliment, whether he intended it to be or not, that I have ever or will ever receive. My son said, "Not business-like."

I want to praise my brother Tony for a minute. If you ever hear Tony, pray you will agree - his prayers are not business-like. They aren't the usual "guard, guide, and direct us" prayers. This is especially true when at home. Dad and I were doing some concrete work and I stayed the night with Tony's family. The way Tony prayed with his children astounded me. My niece and nephew are so blessed. Tony speaks to God like a close and admired friend. He speaks to our Father the way I want my own children to come and talk to me. Here is the prayer I prayed that night after the marriage lesson.

"We pray first for ourselves as men. We know we are broken men, sinners. We confess the ugliness of it to you, our hate and bitterness, petty jealousies, and twisted lusts. Let us confess it completely also to those we have hurt. Our spirit is willing, but our flesh is weak.

We are men who want to be men of God, men of integrity. We want to be servants to the weak, to look on our sisters, your daughters, in all purity. We want to love our wives and nurture our daughters with courageous, sacrificial leadership. We want to be men who own our own sins, shifting blame nowhere but on ourselves. And having done so, let us find full forgiveness in the perfect man Jesus. Father, in Your strength, we want to stand as true men.

Make us a nation full of men who build up a safe, protective wall around those you have entrusted to our care, who then go out and stand in the gap as watchful shepherds and unflinching warriors. Father, I'll ask one thing more for myself and my brothers. We know a servant does not deserve gratitude because he does his job, but still, fill with gratitude the hearts of these men who serve. Let kind words sprinkle these men like cool rain after hard work, a hot shower after a long day. Let a kind word of thanks, a look of appreciation, or a light touch refresh the spirit of these men so they get back up, go out, and give that same devoted service tomorrow.

We pray for our sisters, your daughters. May they find and come to know their true value in Jesus. They are valuable, every one of your daughters, because You treasure them. The young and old alike. Mothers and single women. Widows and the childless. They matter to You, and they matter to us. They are the joy in joyful homes. They have such power to build homes and churches and communities. God help them understand the overwhelming power they have to build homes and to encourage all the lives around them, or to tear them down with her own hands. It is strength no man has.

They are our wives, our sisters, our mothers, and our daughters. They enrich our lives in ways that cannot be quantified with dollars. It's true, You spoke the truth, their value is far above rubies. It's at their tables we eat and laugh and share life. It's by the work of their caring hands that we are comforted. Let them do this honorable work, let them respect their husbands and fathers without fear.

We both, men and women, have acted out of fear of losing control and giving up power. We strive for sovereignty. We've abused one another mutually. It's all sinful. Destructive. We know that you visit the misdeeds of parents on the children and grandchildren. We pass bad habits down - toxic, sinful behaviors - as inheritances. You also bless those who love you for generations to follow. Teach us the better way." - Amen

Tell Me that Story Again

I spent some time tonight with an elderly brother in Christ. He is a widower twice over and mostly home bound. His second wife passed more than a year ago and every time I visit him, he reflects on his wives. He tells me how they met, where they dated, where they lived. He reminisces about their own individual charms, and he talks about how he lost them. I'm not inclined to say much about marriage, especially not mine. I'm divorced. I still trust that God's design is the best and happiest for men and women, but it is refreshing to hear an old man describe the women he loved for the best part of his life and that he still cherishes them. In fact, every time I visit, I hope he tells me those same stories again.

Can We Still Reach the Next Generation?

What do the millennials want? What can we do to make them interested in spiritual matters? This week I saw a series of comments on social media offering such advice as: Passion over passive; Relevant over boring; Doers over talkers; Mission over money; and Love over apathy. Catchy, but I wonder... is a new technique or philosophy of evangelism needed to reach our children and grandchildren? Is one generation really that different from another? Millennials and Zoomers want passionate doers and a mission motivated by love; how is that different from the seventeen-year-old Baby Boomer of the sixties?

If one truth has stood out over and over in our study of the Old Testament here in Robinson, it is this - people are still people. We may speak a different language, be separated by thousands of miles and thousands of years, but we have the same fears, worries, and motives that moved people in the Bible. Rather than asking what millennials want, the helpful question is - what is the Scripture's model of generational teaching?

Grab the attention. When Israel stood at the foot of Sinai, God grabbed their attention (Heb 12:18-29). In Luke, Jesus teaches the Parable of the Sower, explains it to the disciples privately, then warns them to "take care how you listen" (Lk 8:18). Yes, be careful to what you listen to, but in this verse, Jesus says "how" you listen. Did the disciples hear Jesus? They'd say "yes, of course!" But like many of us who have heard countless sermons, could their attention have drifted out the window? Might they have started counting lines in the paneling? I may be a minister, but I've daydreamed through plenty of sermons in my life, too. After this, Jesus drifted to sleep in a boat when a storm cameon the sea. The disciples, scared to death, roused Jesus. You can read the rest of the story, but let me ask you a question - did Jesus have their attention now?

Be a true believer. Why did the gospel message spread so powerfully in the first century? Was it wholly the miracles? When I read Acts, I see apostles and Christians who are true believers. They were fearful in the gospels. Fear is a major theme in Mark's gospel and in all four gospels, the apostles abandon Jesus. In Acts, however, Peter is no longer a crumbling pile of gravel but an immovable rock. Jesus nicknamed him that for a reason, you know, and it was true of all the men (Ac 2:32; 3:15).

Most Christians were genuine, honest, and passionate. Not everyone was though - there were false brethren (2 Cor 11:26; Gal 2:4). And even genuine Christians were not perfect in everything all the time. Paul's letter to the Corinthians should be evidence enough to prove that. But those who were genuine, honest, and passionate truly were. Paul was. Here's how he spoke - "the goal of our instruction is love from a pure heart and a good conscience and a sincere faith" (1 Tim 1:5). "For to me, to live is Christ" (Phil 1:21). "For we are not like many, peddling the word of God, but as from sincerity, but as from God, we speak in Christ in the sight of God" (2 Cor 2:17). Were these empty platitudes? Righteous rhetoric? Church speak? No. It was true believers like Paul who, by their genuine and honest passion for Christ, sowed the same in others.

It hurts me when I think of people, some so close to me, who do not share my faith. Perhaps the seed is still germinating in their heart. That is my belief and most prayed for hope. But I am confident not one of them would accuse me of just towing a line, parroting a script, or wearing a mask. "Oh God, may the genuineness of my convictions be a catalyst for Your word to blossom in those around me."

On this matter of being a true believer I want to say something about professional ministers. Paul wrote, "We are not like many, peddling the word of God." And Amos, "I am not a prophet, nor am I the son of a prophet...But the Lord took me...and the Lord said to me, 'Go prophesy to My people' (Amos 7:14, 15). I always feel a little funny referencing that passage. It's true - my dad is a preacher and on first meeting, some folks may assume I've followed in the "family brininess." But I detest the spirit of professional preachers.

What do I mean? I do a lot of speaking and have worked to develop that skill, but I'm not a spokesman, salesman, or pitchman. I don't sell Jesus or His church. I am paid for preaching but I am not a hireling. No matter how the IRS classifies me, I am not a church employee just as I do not view the Christians I worship with to be bosses. They are my brothers, and I am theirs. I know other preachers. I have their numbers in my phone. Sometimes I even meet up with them. But, I do not attend meetings, conferences, or lectureships for the purpose of networking.

I suppose one way to illustrate what I'm trying to describe is through the kinship of preaching and politics. I know... the comparison is distasteful to me too, but sometimes the best medicine tastes the worst. In politics, there are men and women who are career politicians There are others in politics who are public servants. "For we do not preach ourselves but Christ Jesus as Lord, and ourselves as your bond-servants for Jesus' sake" (2 Cor 4:5).

.

The Most Effective Outreach Program

My dad's father left home and school after eighth grade. He packed all his belongings in a small cardboard suitcase and moved north to make money cutting broomcorn. He was in Korea for his twenty-first birthday and when the army turned him loose, he came back to farm here in Illinois. He had an opportunity to take a class on farm business through the government, and on the first day of the class, the instructor came in and announced to the men that he would introduce them to the most valuable piece of equipment they could purchase for their farms. He proceeded to take from his pocket a yellow number 2 pencil.

Grandma told me this story. She had found a bunch of grandpa's old papers in his desk after he passed. Showing them to me, she commented that he was always figuring, always running numbers. You see, my grandpa took his teacher's words to heart. He calculated buying land, what the return would be, or would it be wiser to purchase a tractor. I don't know what all he was figuring, but he wore through pencils due to careful planning.

I miss that man. I wish I could have grown up farming with him. I think about him often even though he's been with the Lord seventeen years. I think about simple life lessons he exemplified, like the one about the pencil.

I'm a minister but I think there is some overlap in his story. I have tools for my work- shelves of books. I'm an old school guy; my library isn't digital. I have a computer. It's useful for publishing things like this bulletin and PowerPoint enhances my sermons. I have preaching friends who are far more tech savvy than I am. Ministers and farmers aren't that dissimilar. We all like the new, the shiny, the latest sophisticated tools. Ministers, church leaders, even Christian parents keep looking for new and better ways to reach another generation.

Don't get me wrong. I am not opposed to using technology and developing new skills in teaching.But remember - never be so infatuated with the latest and greatest that you snub your nose at the basic. Computers and iPads and jumbo smart TVs do not make Christians. Podcasts and lecture series and seeker sensitive outreach programs will not convert the world.

Sheep make sheep. It's just that simple. Don't be so distracted by the new and shiny that you forget this basic biblical truth. Like produces after its kind. Christians make Christians. You can have the latest gear, the most popular program, but if you don't have a Christian with a genuine faith in God and the Scriptures, what will your programs really create?

"Behold, the sower went out to sow" (Mt 13:3).

Coffee Filters

No K-Cups for me. None of those frou-frou frappuccinos either. Just give me plain old Folgers, black and stout. You can enjoy what you like, but this is how I usually make coffee in the morning. My daughter used to make it when she lived at home... so strong we teased her that a stirring spoon would stand to attention. I was thinking about that the other morning while pouring the grounds in the coffee maker. Like my daughter, I don't tend to measure much in the kitchen. Anyway, I had peeled off a single filter from the stack and set it in the machine and noticed that the stack was getting a bit thin. I don't really know how many filters come in a package when I buy them, but it sure seems like a lot. Peel one off and it doesn't look any less than before. The next time, too, and the time after that. Week after week. But then one day, like the other morning, you see it. You're finally aware of it - I'm running low.

This thought isn't new with me. I remember reading in a religious journal a few years ago (I can't recall which one or the author's name) but he made this point about coffee filters, and I still think about it at times while making a few cups in the morning. What does our life stack up to, seventy or eighty years (Ps 90:10)? How many days is that? A lot. An inexhaustible bounty when you're just a boy or girl. In your teens and twenties, the stack is still so numerous. Even at middle age, there's plenty left. The supply is noticeably less than it used to be, but there's still a lot.

I don't know how a person might ruin a coffee filter, but I suppose if you did, it wouldn't be any great concern to just pull off another. Each one is so inexpensive, the loss of one so inconsequential. But how many days have you peeled off your life, ruined or just wasted?

"Teach us to consider our mortality, so that we might live wisely" (Ps 90:12 NET). This doesn't mean, and I am not implying, that every day should be packed as full as we can stuff it with activity. When you try to do ten different things at once, you don't do any one of them well. I had an old Scoutmaster who liked to say: "a man's day should be eight hours of work, eight of play, and eight of rest." I think there is wisdom in that.

Live well the days God has blessed you. Perhaps today is time for worship, prayer, and meditating on God's word. Maybe tomorrow is time to sweat and earn a living. Maybe another day is time for investing in or repairing relationships.

On a few occasions, I have run out of coffee filters. Cowboy coffee is a good way to go, but it takes some practice. Once I tried reusing the same filter from the day before. It was a little messy, but it worked okay. I'd like to rerun, reuse, and live again some of those days when my daughter was home making coffee. There are several others I'd like to drink from again too, but we all know a day is single use only. Live this one well.

Cucumbers & Ministry

It's just a tiny little thing. Sprouted up so nice in the early summer; put out a few leaves. Then they all turned brown, withered, and fell off. What happened to my little cucumber plant? I really like garden cucumbers, so this was a major issue. I had prepared the raised bed with good compost, mulched the little green thing just right, and watered it well. Why was it dying? Some other plants were growing a little slow, but they were still obviously alive. Taking a careful look, down near the root, something had damaged my little cucumber plant. It was hurt and fragile but still alive.

I've nursed that little sprout morning and night. Watering carefully enough but not too strong of a shower. I don't want the roots washed away. Mulch it a little more to keep the roots moist. And sure enough - a new leaf once again sprouted! I don't expect this little plant will be the one to keep me stocked in pickles this year, but I saw a single flower on it today.

Ministry is so much like nursing little plants. Ministry - not preaching in pulpits -is Christians serving one another. Some people will hear the gospel, receive it willingly, gladly, and take off faithfully after obeying it. Others need patient and careful attention. Gentle hands. Patient voices. Regular care. "Preach the word with great patience" (2 Tim 4:2).

We are not professionals. We are ministers. Servants of one another. We may be a little too rough with one, water another too lightly. We may overlook some and they begin to fade. Just take note and be more thoughtful. Keep nursing it along. If it is green, it's still alive and worth your time.

Island Dweller

Jesus came to save. Some people ask:"What about all the people who have never heard about Him or the gospel?" Well, I'm sure you have heard this scripture before: "'Whoever will call on the name of the Lord will be saved.' How then will they call on Him in whom they have not believed? How will they believe in Him whom they have not heard? And how will they hear without a preacher" (Rom 10:13-14)?

Imagine that there is a man on some remote undiscovered island. How did he get there? I don't know. How long has he lived there all alone? Again, I don't know. Maybe you have heard hypothetical questions like this before. The point is that this man has never heard about Jesus and supposedly never will. Now what do you think, will this man be lost? God is good. He is fair. How could he condemn this man? "Shall not the Judge of all the earth deal justly" (Gen 18:25)?

In answering this question, our emotions can easily drive our thinking and end up taking us to unscriptural places. So let me offer a follow-up hypothetical situation for the island dweller. Suppose one day the man is fishing a little way from shore. A wave rolls in and catches him by surprise. He stumbles, falls, and the current pulls him out farther. He tries swimming back to shore, but the tide is too strong and he soon fatigues. He drowns. Is it unfair? Unjust? Not right? Why did he drown? We might think he drowned because no one was there to save him, but that really isn't the reason. He drowned because he was in the water.

People are lost because they are drowning in sin. The scriptures teach, "The person who sins will die" (Eze 18:20). "Your iniquities have made a separation between you and your God, and your sins have hidden His face from you" (Isa 59:2). And further, "For the wages of sin is death" (Romans 3:23). Every person who is lost, whether they have heard the gospel or not, is lost because they are sinners. That may feel uncomfortable and hard to hear, but it is the truth. Another truth is that God does not want any person to be lost (2 Pet 3:9), though many do reject him. Jesus came "to seek and to save that which was lost" (Lk 19:10). He sent the disciples to share the gospel with the world (Lk 24:47). And in His love, God will not force anyone to live with Him forever. It's foolish, but a drowning man is free to reject a lifeline when it's thrown to him.

A second biblical truth we need to remember is that God is not hiding from anyone. Jesus said, "Seek and you shall find" (Matt 7:7). The creation itself bears witness to the Creator (Rom 1:19-20). Even a man stranded alone on an island can observe that. If this man wanted to know his creator, I am convinced by the promise of Jesus that he would find God. How? I can't say how God may work. He may allow a Christian to be shipwrecked and stranded with the man. God sent preachers before. He sent Philip to the Ethiopian (Acts 8) and Peter to Cornelius (Acts 10). If you are worried over the lost who have never heard of Jesus, then do what Jesus taught us to do. Go make disciples (Matt 28:19). Seek them out. Maybe in God's providence, a Bible in a bottle washes up on the man's shore. I know it seems farfetched—nothing like that could happen, right? But don't you believe the Bible yourself? "With God all things are possible" (Matt 19:26).

What A Waste

"Brian had sorted through the few belongings he had with him. He was alone and cold and the comforts of his suburban life had been stripped away. He was facing reality, harsh and unbending. He took the twenty-dollar bill from his wallet and began carefully cutting it into strips."

It's been a long time since I was first introduced to Brian in Gary Paulsen's book, Hatchet. It is the story of a young boy stranded in the Canadian wild after the small plane he was on crashed. I loved the book so much as a child that when I found a copy at a thrift store a few years ago, I eagerly bought it and read it with my children. One of the eye-opening moments for Brian comes when he tries to make a fire. He could get a spark from striking his hatchet on a rock but needed something smaller than twigs to catch it. This is when he takes the twenty from his wallet. In his old life back home, this printed paper had value (and much more back in the 80's when Paulsen published the book.) I don't think I'd ever even held a twenty when I first read the book; it was a lot of money, in my young opinion. Brian looked at it. He couldn't eat it. He couldn't clothe himself with it. It was worthless. It was just paper...so why not try to burn it? He shredded it and, just to enforce the lesson that his old way of thinking/his old value system must die, the torn up twenty won't even burn.

Let me draw out a comparison. I don't want to think that I am wasting my life. I'm frugal with money. I take care to maintain my vehicles and make them last. I have postponed fun to work and save and get ahead. No, of course I'm not wasteful, but I read in Isaiah, "Why do you spend money for what is not bread, and your wages for what does not satisfy? Listen carefully to Me, and eat what is good" (Isa 55:2). The Lord says to the well-situated man, "You fool! This very night your soul is required of you; and now who will own what you have prepared" (Lk 12:20)?

Are we sure we aren't hording up trash? Paul says, "I count all things to be loss in view of the surpassing value of knowing Christ Jesus my Lord, for whom I have suffered the loss of all things and count them but rubbish so that I may gain Christ" (Phil 3:8). Are you sure we aren't spending precious days buying up and gobbling down shadows of food? What a waste.

Looking again to Isaiah, the Lord offers in the verse just before the one mentioned above, "Everyone who thirsts, come to the waters; and you who have no money come, buy and eat. Come, buy wine and milk without money and without cost." The best of life, those things that have real value, God gives freely. Not just the necessities, such as water, but luxuries like wine and milk in abundance (Isa 55:1).

It Was Pride

It was one of my greatest fears. It had kept me from doing the good I knew I should do. No one had asked me to write a church bulletin here. I could have left the entire project alone, but I have the time. I have ability. I wanted to do more to build up the church. I had (I thought) good intentions, but pride was in the way.

Let me clarify. This is especially important with sins like pride. It puts on the mask of humility so easily. You see, I don't think I'm superior. I'm not the greatest preacher. I'm not the best writer or thinker. The truth is, I know I am deficient in so much. That's not false humility; it's just true.

Pride was not an issue for me because I thought I was better than others.Rather the opposite. I struggle so much with spelling. No matter how much I proofread, I still don't catch everything. It's embarrassing. When I was a young preacher, the older brother I was training with would take my bulletin drafts. After catching every misspelling, typo, or grammatical error, he would proceed to give me a weekly spelling test like I was in second grade again. It was humiliating. I have strong feelings about that brother and that experience. I remember preaching years later about a sermon entitledHeavenly Things with an emphasis on angels. On my PowerPoint slides, however, I had typed, "angles." Not just once, but on every slide. The church laughed. I don't blame them. It was funny the first time. It was just sad after a few more.

I share those memories only to demonstrate that I am very sensitive to spelling issues. I hate feeling like I am stupid, and I knew if I started writing a bulletin every week, there would be mistakes. So, I put it off for years. That was pride. I was more focused on myself, worried about what people would think of me, than serving God.

Remember what Jesus says to Paul about his thorn in the flesh? "My grace is sufficient for you, for power is perfected in weakness." And Paul continues, "Most gladly, therefore, I will rather boast about my weaknesses, so that the power of Christ may dwell in me. Therefore, I am well content with weaknesses...for when I am weak, then I am strong" (2 Cor 12:9–10).

I'm not advocating ignorance. I'm not anti-intellectual. I'm against pride. Even when pride is rooted to my weaknesses, it's still pride because I am elevating my appearance, my reputation, my look above my Lord.

They Had a Name

It seems to go on forever. The Wall. I was looking down the length of the Vietnam WarTraveling Memorial when it was in Danville, Kentucky several years ago. I'd seen pictures of it. You probably have, too, but like with many things, pictures never do it justice.

I didn't realize until that day the purposeful visual impact designed into the memorial. The portable monument tapers down at both ends. I had always assumed from pictures that it was just, well, a wall. The monument in Washington uses the natural valley in the landscape to create the visual effect I was experiencing. There are 58,318 names etched on the wall and when you stand next to it and look down its length it appears to go on forever to the horizon. Like a tragic movie's end credits playing on and on infinitum.

I was with a friend that day. He is my dad's age, and he spent a little time looking for the name of one of his school mates among those fifty-eight thousand names. I've been to the Harold Washington Library in Chicago where fifty-eight thousand dog tags hang from the ceiling as a memorial. It's called Above and Beyond. I remember expecting to hear slight clinks of metal because the dog tags all hung closely together. But the monument isn't a wind chime. They hang side by side. In columns. In rows. Mustered together and standing at attention. Each tag weighs only a few grams but a crushing burden together.

There is another image I've seen a few times. It's a graph representing all the casualties of all the wars through all the years of the United States' existence. Sometimes the graph employs crosses to represent 10,000 dead. Sometimes it is simply a red line that increases in length as the numbers climb. Finally, as the devastating human toll of war slows another line begins to grow... a line that only began growing at the end of the Vietnam War. It's a line that has grown only for fifty years, a fifth of America's history. But it grows beyond that of forgotten wars. It stretches out further than the Civil War, beyond the Great War, past World War Two. It dwarfs Korea and Vietnam and all the conflicts in the middle east. It passes them all, but it doesn't stop growing. Longer and longer it goes until all the casualties of all the wars all together are minuscule in comparison. Sixty-three million... one thousand Vietnams.

There is a monument in Washington dedicated to the young men sacrificed in Vietnam. Do you know what the difference is between those soldiers and the sixty-three million babies sacrificed at the altar of convenience since 1973? The boys that died in Vietnam had names.

She's Nice

You know about the virtuous woman of Proverbs, right? The woman described at the end of the book. Do you remember the other woman of Proverbs, the one described in chapter seven?

"With her many persuasions she entices him; With her flattering lips she seduces him...he does not know that it will cost him his life" (Pr 7:21–23). She's boisterous, aggressive, and cunning. She's quite the sight, dressed as she is.

I've always thought this woman was obvious. She must have a wicked smile. She's bad and looks like trouble. That's how the dad of proverbs portrays her.

I'm a dad too, and if I've learned a few things about relationships and women, if I've earned the right to speak into a young man's life, I'd want him to know this—she's sometimes really nice. She's shy. She's sweet. Feminine. If there were such a thing as a soul mate, she'd make you think you'd found yours. She's not manipulative, but like the woman of Proverbs 7, she has no right to be with you. She's bound to another.

My son, if I've earned your trust even a little, believe me, she's nice. She'll make you think of abandoning everything. Everything—your integrity, your family, your job, and future. You'll contemplate leaving it all for a whirlwind summer romance.

You'll want to lay aside responsibilities and put down your cross for just a little bit. Take a break from always being good. You'll rationalize. You'll avoid friends who you know will counsel you to do what you already know to be right. If you still talk with God, you'll plead for it to be another way.

My son, I know.She's nice, but she'll lead you to the same place as the wicked one.

You Take Care Of You

I don't remember it happening too often, but often enough, I remember these words of hers. It may have been while my brothers and I fought. Fighting is probably too strong a description. Playing in the yard would usually turn into wrestling and naturally, wrestling turned more spirited. So, whatever you would call that is what we did. Mom babysat a few children, too, so there were always lots of kids around and disagreements would spark. Eventually someone not involved would run off and tattle. I must have been the tattletale a few times for me to remember mom's words at this point in the senecio - "I'll mind them, you just take care of you."

Modern helicopter parents may not agree with my mother's approach (and I don't have space in this article to expand on parenting styles), but I lean toward supervision not suffocation. I do want to make a connection, however, to our relationship with fellow Christians.

Jesus warned about false prophets (Matt 7:15-20). Paul, Peter, Jude, and John all did likewise (2 Tim 3:1-5; 2 Pet 2:1; Jude 3-4; 1 Jn 4:1-3). There are examples in Scripture of these false teachers and false brethren being pointed out and even named (2 Tim. 2:17, 4:14; 3 Jn. 9). I want to be clearly heard and understood that I believe sin, error, and the unfruitful deeds of darkness should be exposed (Eph 5:11). There is, however, another spiritual reality that I must acknowledge—I am not law enforcement. The Scriptures call on me to humble myself before God (Jas 4:10), or in my words, accept your place in His order. Further, the Scriptures warn me about passing judgment on other Christians because only a judge can pass sentence and there is only room for one judge. Jesus has already filled that position. This only leaves me the job of doer of the law as a law-abiding citizen (Jas 4:11-12). How do we balance what James teaches with equally clear instruction about error, sin, and false teaching?

In my little town, if you come in from the west on the state road there is a large sign low to the ground. The local speed limit is 35mph and our local officer likes to park his cruiser behind this sign. He is looking to catch people speeding. (Fair warning, if you come to Palestine, Illinois - mind your speed.) Now, I won't be sitting along the road with a radar gun myself. I'll not be watching from my living room window, intent on reporting every heavy foot that comes down my street. Likewise, I don't view my purpose as a Christian to be sheriff or hall monitor of the church, certainly not of the brotherhood. I can't write tickets. I don't have the authority. As a man who doesn't like paying fees to the county, however, I'll warn you about breaking the speed limit here.

It Builds Character

"It builds character." Dad used to say this to my brothers and me when he had some chore for us to do. I'm sure he heard it from his dad and my children hear it from me. It's one of those dad-isms that cause kids to groan and cringe. (Dads, keep saying them anyway.) Another more modern version is this - "Hard times create strong men. Strong men create good times. Good times create weak men. Weak men create hard times."

And what exactly is a strong man? The physically chiseled gym bro is just as empty as the emotionally sensitive, in-touch-with-his-feminine-side, feminist model. Robert Bly describes the evolution and degeneration of modern masculinity into the "soft male" in his book Iron John. He writes, "They're lovely, valuable people—I like them—they're not interested in harming the earth or starting wars. There's a gentle attitude toward life in their whole being and style of living. But many of these men are not happy. You quickly notice the lack of energy in them. They are life-preserving but not exactly life-giving. Ironically, you often see these men with strong women who positively radiate energy. Here we have a finely tuned young man, ecologically superior to his father, sympathetic to the whole harmony of the universe, yet he himself has little vitality to offer."

In past years, I've read the Psalms while thoughtfully meditating on David's prayers. Struggle is a reoccurring theme in them. David is afflicted by enemies or suffering from some difficulty, and he prays for deliverance. I pray for the same myself, but I wonder then, why David never seems to enjoy an easy, peaceful life. David's troubles seem to come like ocean waves, as soon as one rolls out, in crashes another. Psalm 55 is one of these typical prayers. Consider the ending, "Cast your burden upon the Lord and he will sustain you; He will never allow the righteous to be shaken/moved." Strong men are steady men, made so by challenge, acting with unshakable character.

Is an easy life really what we want? For all of those who work jobs they hate, or that stress them out, think back to the spring of 2020. Many people got their wish during the lockdowns when they no longer had to go to work. How fast did the fun and happiness wear off? Being left with nothing to do but watch Netflix became its own kind of torment.

Men need difficulties. They need challenges to thrive. Not so much that they are crushed, but enough pressure to focus them. David faced one difficulty after another and God's answer was not to give him an easy life void of problems, but the assurance to keep moving steadily along saying, "I'll see you through this one too."

A final note, I'd similarly encourage my daughters to be strong women. The world has more than enough princesses; it needs more pioneers. As I heard Jordan Peterson, a fellow father say, "Find the largest burden you can bear and bear it." It builds character.

Worthy of the Gospel

I have a picture of my daughter when she was small. She might have been six or seven. She had a butterfly that had lighted on her face and as the picture was taken, it took flight. She looked up. Her face was bright and her blonde hair a-swirling. Smiling. If you were to see this picture you would immediately know so much about my precious little girl. Full of joy and wonder. That one photo captures her personality as much as it does her image. It does justice to her. It's a worthy picture.

No one deserves God's mercy, or Jesus' sacrifice, but that is not what the New Testament means when it calls us to live "worthy of the gospel" (Phil 1:27; Eph 4:1; Col 1:10; 1 Ths 2:12). Living worthy of the gospel means living in a way that reflects its truth and love and grace. Living gospel worthy is doing justice to the gospel's hope and forgiveness. In Philippians, Paul goes on to mention three aspects of the gospel as he asks a few rhetorical questions. "Therefore, if there is any encouragement in Christ, if there is any consolation of love, if there is any fellowship of the Spirit, if any affection and compassion, make my joy complete by being of the same mind, maintaining the same love, united in spirit, intent on one purpose" (Phil 2:1-2).

Does the gospel offer encouragement? Sure, it does! I might say that outside the hope of the gospel, what encouragement really is there? Does the gospel console or can it provide fellowship and unity? Again, yes!And what consoles better than the hope of resurrection? What binds tighter than the family of God? If these are so, then be courageous, be comforting, and be united with God's people. Live in a way that does justice to the gospel and the God who called you through it.

Living Blessed is Messy

You've heard the adage - "you can't bake a cake without breaking a few eggs." It conveniently can be applied to many situations, so I'll borrow it too. The good life, the life that can reflect and say, "God, has richly blessed me," is messy.

I began thinking about it this week while visiting some friends in Kentucky. On Friday evening, after dinner, the father of the family read Proverbs 14:4, "Where there are no oxen, the manger is clean, but abundant crops come by the strength of the ox."

I'm a good house guest; I think they would agree. I straighten the bed sheets before I leave and fold my bath towel. I don't leave candy wrappers between the sofa cushions, and though I don't take off my boots at the door, I do try not to track in mud. Still, I know my visiting makes some mess and a little extra work for them. I'd like to think they enjoy my company and so don't mind my little mess making.

Similarly, my sister's family is coming over today. We both know the house will be messy. Honestly, it starts messy, but gets more so when all the family is in. Today I plan to fuss around in the kitchen and make lunch. Dirty up dishes. The kids will make noise and run to find toys and play. Tonight, we'll drag out all the blankets and make up beds on the floor. In the morning, we'll whip up pancakes and make more mess. And here is what I'm going to do about it...thank God for it. Love every minute of it. When they all leave, I can clean the kitchen and fold the blankets. I'll have all the peace and quiet I can stand in a big and empty house. Living blessed is messy.

It was a sad realization years ago when I stood up to preach one morning and noticed that there was not one spit-up stain on the lapel of my sport coat. After years of crusty milk stains, there was now no more mess because I didn't have babies to hold anymore. Living blessed is messy.

An old brother here in Robinson used to say during closing announcements, "I just love to hear those babies when they cry out." Moms and dads, I know you try to pacify and keep those children quiet, but babies get fussy sometimes. So what if they are being distracting! You know what's worse than the mess and noise of babies? A church with none. I'd thank God for some crying babies. Lord, give us some noise; give us some mess here.

Have you thought about babes in Christ? Seeing people confess their faith and be baptized is exciting until the longtime churchgoers realize that these infant Christians aren't baby dolls. Their smiles aren't painted on. The clothes aren't always neat; their hair isn't perfectly curled. They are messy. They have ungodly habits and behaviors like ways of dressing, speaking, and responding to attacks. While being sanctified they, like the Corinthian Christians, stumble when trying to walk. Do you feel like these "messy" disciples hold you back or slow down the work? You know what is worse than a chaotic church full of immature new converts with messy lives? The peaceful tranquility of a dead church. I'll say it again - living blessed is messy. God, I pray for some messy people.

You'll Make a Good Wife

Sometimes I wonder if I'm doing okay by my children, raising them right and all. I think I was given some good insight today.

We were having some people over for lunch after worship, so I was busy cooking early this morning when one of the girls smelled the ham and said, "Aw Pa, you'll make a good wife one day." While you're laughing at that just know, I happen to have a very good book written by a preacher's wife titled Just Get a Ham. Anyway, after lunch my girls jumped right in to help wash up the dishes and I mentioned something about us using some of my grandma's crystal dishes. My daughter Megan asked what would happen to them when I'm gone. I said, "Well, I reckon you'll have to take them and put them to use." She wiped dry the platter she was holding with her towel and said, "I'd rather have your guns."

I think we are doing okay. She's a fair cook and more than a fair shot.

I Thought You Knew

Assumptions are dangerous. I don't know how many times I must relearn this same old lesson before it will stick with me, but I've been shown it again. Just because something is old and familiar to me doesn't mean it is the same to others. I'm sure that is true for many things. Old bands gain new fans as younger generations find their music. Scriptural truth is like this too. Peter says, "I will always be ready to remind you of these things, even though you already know them, and have been established in the truth which is present with you...And I will also be diligent that at any time after my departure you will be able to call these things to mind" (1 Pet 1:12, 15).

I've had church members complain that my preaching was too simplistic. "There just isn't any meat." As feedback goes, complaints are rare. Compliments are more common and much appreciated. This past week someone commended my sermons on the book of Revelation for their simplicity. He said they weren't what he expected but were helpful none the less. Still, that one complaint (as negative words tend to do) has stuck with me. I've felt guilty of being lazy when giving a sermon on bible basics – basics about salvation; basics about worship; basics about how the church is organized or functions. Just basic sermons, the kind of sermons I preached when I was just a kid. I worry about them boring people. I think to myself - they've heard these things all before.

This past week I was speaking with a teenager. Though I won't divulge the whole scenario, I'll just acknowledge that based on the number of sermons they've heard throughout their life, I just thought they knew certain truths (basic truths, in my mind.) They are struggling with faith and the inconsistent behavior they see in some Christians. Now, after reflecting on our talk, I think a lot of their confusion is based in ignorance. They simply do not know the truth on some issues. I think I will write them a letter. I can be careful how I phrase what I will say to them, but they need to hear the truth. Be gracious (Col 4:6). Let love motivate your words (Eph 4:15) but be honest and tell the truth. Like Jesus said, "you will know the truth, and the truth will make you free" (Jn 8:32). Light scatters the darkness. It exposes error and drives away ignorance. I thought you knew. It was an assumption, and it was wrong.

Back to the business of preaching basic sermons. Do you know how often my mom made mashed potatoes for supper when I was a boy? I could sooner count the times she didn't. It may have been the same meal over and over, but mom made it fresh each time. You can preach bible basics, just don't let them be the TV dinners of sermons.

A Prized Preacher

"Receive [Epaphroditus] then in the Lord with all joy, and hold men like him in high regard" (Ph 2:29).

In context, Epaphroditus had come close to death, risking his life for Christ and the Philippians. Paul is right - we ought to hold such men in high regard. There are men I know, I'm sure you do too, who have been in dangerous places preaching Jesus. The service of their families should not be overlooked either. Others have served and generously given even to their impoverishment, saving up treasures in heaven. God is sure to reward them, but like Paul says, we should esteem them, and I think we do.

I want to shift the direction of our thinking on this subject just a little. What do you or your church or the brotherhood esteem most about men in the pulpit? Some of the men I admire are very smart. Many are also highly educated. Do you think we sometimes aren't so smart though and confuse the two?

Some of the men I admire are bold and confident. They inspire and encourage me to preach without fear. I wonder though, if we get confidence confused with competence. Do you think because someone is loud, passionate, and sure of themselves they must know what they're talking about? Many have been fooled by this before.

Some of the men I admire have beautiful families. They are happy and loving, close knit, and devout. They refresh my spirit when I spend time with them. What do you think then about Jesus, Paul, the prophets, and apostles? What did their family pictures look like?

My Sunday Best

It's Sunday so I'll polish my boots, press my shirt, and make sure my gig line is straight, but the best-looking men always dress in self-respect, courage, and integrity.

Weeds

The struggle is never ending. I'll clean up a patch of garden space one day and a few days later, the weeds are back. Dandelions, purslane, wood sorrel, pokeweed, nettles, creeping charlie, and lambsquartar. A friend asked me, "How's your garden looking this year, Ray?" "Well," I responded, "I sure can grow a healthy crop of weeds."

Some years I just go with it and let the weeds grow too. After all, a lot of them have uses. Wood sorrel has a nice lemon taste and I do like the little yellow flowers. Lambsquarter is a lazy gardener's spinach. I have some purslane relish I made last year. Oh, and milkweed!It smells like lilac and monarch butterflies lay their eggs on it. Tastes a bit like asparagus when young, but don't confuse it with wild asparagus. One of my favorite useful weeds is called broadleaf. Some people call it plantain. I love its colloquial name. Others know it as white-man's footprint. It's not native to the Americas, but it started sprouting up everywhere Europeans began to settle (so the story goes.)

It's well-known for its medicinal uses, both the leaves and the seeds, but it's terribly ugly and it grows everywhere. Unless you've made serious effort to eradicate it, you have it in your yard. It grows in gravel driveways, abandoned lots, even cracks in the pavement. It's like the cockroach of the plant world.

You may find this to be an awful comparison, but this weed is an accurate illustration of God's kingdom. Jesus compared the kingdom to a mustard seed, that some considered a weed, and to yeast, that often represents contamination (Matt 13:31-33). I like this comment by Ken Chumbly, "That Christ should use it (a mustard seed and leaven) to describe the kingdom is analogous to using rust or a virus for the same purpose."

Everywhere Christians go, churches spring up. The seed (Lk 8:11), being the gospel message, first sown in Jerusalem in the hearts of just a few committed disciples soon covered the known world because "those who were scattered went on their way preaching the word" (Ac 8:4).

Christianity is rugged. It's hardy. It can't be plucked from the world by persecution. "The gates of Hades will not overpower it" (Mt 16:18). Spray it with skepticism and materialism. Eradicate it in one place. The church will simply come back next year, with the next generation, or break out and flourish in some other place. Hypocritical leaders trample it with their boots, still the good seed is kicked and carried along. "Some preach Christ out of envy and rivalry, but others out of good will...What does it matter? Only that in every way, whether from false motives or true, Christ is proclaimed, and in this I rejoice" (Phi 1:15, 18).

It's useful, too. The church is no summer rose—pretty to look at for a few days. Some are tampering with the genetics, trying to engineer God's weed into something more aesthetically pleasing. These mutant hybrids, however, have traded all the healing properties for a fleeting pop of color. Worship has morphed into a production, an event. Pop music and inspirational slogans are in full bloom, but where is the demonstration of the spirit and power of God to transform lives (1 Cor 2:4)?

The church, Christianity, the gospel... it's a weed. No doubt the enemies of God will agree, but so do I. It's unstoppable, abundant, and beneficial.

Jesus Wasn't Nice

If you think Jesus was a nice guy, I think you have misunderstood Him. That's a jolting statement I know, but really, why do you think Jesus was a nice guy? What do you mean by "nice"?

I don't think Jesus was cruel. He was gentle (Matt 11:29). His compassion was overflowing (Matt 9). He served and made time for all sorts of people. But when I think of a nice guy, I think of someone who is kind and meek like Jesus, but also someone who avoids conflict at all costs. Someone who may even compromise their integrity to get along with people. Nice guys say whatever is fashionable in present company. Jesus wasn't that.

As sure as Jesus is light and love, He is also the truth (Jn 14:6). He doesn't just tell the truth;He is the embodiment of truth. There is nothing phony about Him, and He never hid what was right to keep from offending people. Do you want some examples? Jesus offended the Pharisees when He told them their worship and practices were a waste of time (Matt 15:12). And I don't think they ever asked His opinion about it, but He told them anyway. Jesus offended a rich young man when He told him he would have to give up the things he treasured to follow Him (Mk 10:22). Jesus even offended people who were devoted to Him. Thousands of people followed Jesus around the countryside, but when He preached a sermon they didn't immediately understand or agree with, they all left Him and went home except the twelve (Jn 6:66).

Yes, Jesus was kind and compassionate to the hurting, but He wasn't silent about sin. He was no nice guy.

Is Your Pantry Full?

When mom and dad lived on the farm, they had a pantry room attached to the kitchen. I was a small guy back then and only remember it because there were saloon door separating the rooms. I wasn't even big enough to kick them open like they do in cowboy movies. Good thing, too, because I imagine mom would not have found my cowboy saunter very funny. Knowing how much mom and dad gardened then, and even later, I would guess that pantry was well-stocked. I inherited mom's canner and in a small basement room lined with shelves, I've tried to carry on the family tradition of a well-stocked pantry.

This morning I was reading in the Gospel of Matthew. At the end of a series of parables, Jesus says, "every teacher of the law who has become a disciple in the kingdom is like the owner of a house who brings out of his storeroom treasures new and old" (Matt 13:52). The verse stood out today because I remembered in the chapter before Jesus rebuked the Pharisees. They frivolously accused Him, and by extension God, as being demonic forces. I hear Jesus respond blunt and quick, "You better watch your mouth; that isn't funny." I'm paraphrasing, but Jesus goes on to add, "A good person produces good things from his storeroom of good, and evil person produces evil things from his storeroom of evil" (Matt 12:35).

I want to confess an uncomfortable truth. As a minister, I have read a lot of the Bible. A lot of it, a lot of times. My reading, however, is always in preparation to teach a class or deliver a sermon. Rarely do I read for my own personal spiritual growth. Everything I take in, I send back out. This shortsightedness finally caught up with me and I felt depleted because I was depleted. My storeroom, my pantry was empty.

A friend and fellow minister encouraged me to make time for reading the scriptures just for myself, just to hear what God is saying. I knew he was right and so I have been doing what he suggested. I do make occasional notes. I think about what I am reading. I'm not just reading to mark off so many chapters daily. No, I am reading intentionally. Not to create a sermon—I guess today's reading did turn into this article. But I am reading to simply hear God, to be filled with His word.

Let me add this before finishing. The world looks much more hopeful now. Just as I'm not worried about going hungry with a full pantry, the more of God's word that is stored up in my heart, the more my heart is at peace. This may be in part due to that fact that the time I had been consuming news and negativity is now used to do my personal daily Scripture reading.

The Hope of the Gospel

If you had just one opportunity, just five minutes let's say, while waiting in line or taking the elevator, what would you say? Imagine you are chatting to the person next to you. The chance to say something about your faith presents itself. What would you say in just a few sentences about Jesus, the gospel, and Christianity?

Almost everyone already knows about Jesus. Some have strong opinions about organized religion and are turned off by it. I personally know some who have grown up going to church and feel like the Bible was "shoved down their throat." Many carry the scars of heavy-handed religious leaders. Many have fled into the temporary comfort of sin only later to find it just as suffocating. What would you say to them? When you can't tell them everything, what's the one thing you want to make sure they hear? I would want them to know that who you were is not who you have to be.

Jesus sets us free. This is the hope of the gospel. It's the promise of God: "Though your sins were red as scarlet, I will make them white as snow" (Isa 1:18). No matter what you have done in the past, Jesus will forgive you. God forgives everyone who repents and will make them a new person, a holy person. You do not have to stay chained to your past mistakes, destined to drag them forever behind you wherever you go. "It was for freedom that Christ set us free" (Gal 5:1). You do not have to be that broken, hurting, lost person forever. There is forgiveness enough for your sins, and mine, and for everyone who will repent. "The grace of our Lord [is] more than abundant" (1 Tim 1:14).

Many of the Christians in the New Testament had lived very wicked lives and they were told: "The unrighteous will not inherit the kingdom of God? Do not be deceived; neither fornicators, nor idolaters, nor adulterers, nor effeminate, nor homosexuals, nor thieves, nor thecovetous, nor drunkards, nor revilers, nor swindlers will inherit the kingdom of God. Such were some of you; but you were washed, but you were sanctified, but you were justified in the name of the Lord Jesus Christ" (1 Cor 6:911).

The world is filled with just two kinds of people. The first kind are sinners who need Jesus, know it, and come to Him for forgiveness. The other kind are likewise sinners who also need Jesus but refuse to humble themselves and accept His forgiveness. You can only be one or the other...so what kind of person will you be?

Practicing Scales

"Learn to play songs, not scales." I don't remember where I heard that, but it's so true. Many children get bored with piano or guitar or whatever instrument because they are taught scales and music theory from the start. They are made to sit and practice scales, up and down, hour after hour. Ugh. I'm bored just thinking about it. Of course, there's value to the fundamentals, but music is so much more than scales.

Let me see if I can make this comparison with Bible study. There is value to knowing the books of the Bible, memorizing verses, and knowing facts. But do not think that being good at Bible trivia is the same as knowing the Scripture. Be "doers of the word and not merely hearers who delude themselves" (Jas 1:22). Faith is far more than knowing facts. I feel I need to add a disclaimer here. I'm not suggesting that we can each make up our own facts, believe whatever we want. Of course not! Just please do not think that filling out workbooks for Sunday school will make a healthy Christian.

Learn to live Christianity. "For to me, to live is Christ" (Phil 1:21). "Everyone who hears these words of Mine and acts on them, may be compared to a wise man who built his house on the rock" (Matt 7:24). Take Christ out of the church building and into the world. Stop singing the Servant Song in the meeting house and be a servant in your own house. I wonder if church, or Christianity as it's promoted, is boring to people because it's just dry facts, intellectual scales striped of rhythm, and feeling.

That's Disgusting

I'm going to relate something disgusting. There's a point to it, so stay with me, but I'm serious, I'm going to tell you something gross first. If you want to skip it, I'll put a marker after this next disgusting part so you'll know when it's over and you can resume reading.

Okay, are you ready? Grandpa had some hogs on his farm. I think they were my uncle's. Anyway, it was summer. My brother and I were out by the hog pens and though they had plenty of water, I turned my head and saw a pig drinking the urine of another. Now that's disgusting and everyone knows it and is disgusted by it except the hogs.

Remember that.

—

In preparation for our Wednesday Bible study in Jeremiah, I was thinking through chapter four. God calls on the people to repent and a condition of this repentance was to put away their idols (Jer 4:1). I paused on this. What's the big deal with idolatry?

When I think of an idol, I have in mind a little statue. Maybe like the gilded plastic figure on a trophy. I've even seen some 4-H trophies topped with a golden sheep or bull. There is nothing disgusting about that. Some people build shelves and set up special display cases for their trophies. Don't misunderstand here. I'm not equating a sport's trophy with idolatry. I'm saying that idolatry and idols are mentioned so much and our understanding of the worship of these false gods is so sanitized that they have become nothing; they even appear to be innocent. God, however, calls them "abhorrent." He calls these idols "disgusting things."

"If a man has sexual intercourse with a male as one has sexual intercourse with a woman, the two of them have committed an abomination" (Lev 20:13 NET). Other sexual perversions are also listed, but this is one that is no longer disgusting to many. Those who practice homosexuality are celebrated, considered stunning and brave. It's cute. Sweet and funny. I don't know, but there might already be a homosexual hallmark Christmas movie playing this season.

More recently the demands that children be prescribed puberty blockers, sex hormones, and possibly even undergo irreversible surgeries to camouflage their binary gender are all being promoted. Parents and grownups are pushing the worship of this disgusting thing.

I hurt for children and adults with gender dysphoria. I hurt for those with same sex attraction. It is a cross some must bear, and their cross is heavy. What is being glorified today, worshipped, and popularized is disgusting. Only the hogs lapping it up can't see how revolting and how truly disgusting it is.

A Prayer

Keep me far from all that is false. Keep my mouth from sharing lies, my ears from entertaining gossip, my eyes from welcoming lust. I renew my covenant today. Keep my heart from filling with pride, my hands from less than my boss expectsand my family deserves. Guard my soul, my body, my mind. Lord, let me walk today in truth. Let my hands be open in charity. Let my heart count the moments of this day quietly. Let me see your image on every face, hear your voice in every verse, and let me confess my sins to you, my faith to the world, and my love to everyone I love. Amen

How God Feels

On Wednesday nights we at Robinson have been thinking through the Old Testament. We cover one or two chapters a week. It took us almost all of last year to work through Isaiah and this year we are reading Jeremiah. Going at this pace has its drawbacks, but one advantage I have found is this time allows the Scriptures to marinate in our minds. The theme of these prophets awakens in our hearts. I really like that word marinate. Yes, I'm describing meditation (Ps 1:2), but I like to think of marinating in God's word, letting it soften and flavor my thinking. More, there are themes in scripture that just require time to sit and stew over. That's my intention as we steadily think through the prophets.

Here are a few themes that stand out to me. First, I'm impressed over and over (everyone at Robinson will attest to this too, because I say it so often in class) people today are no different than people of the past. We may speak a different language, live thousands of miles apart, and have entirely foreign cultures from one another, but the fears and motivations that drove people in Scripture are the same that move people today. This just assures me, and reassures me every time I see it, that the Bible is completely relevant today.

Another is what we saw this past Wednesday evening in Jeremiah. If you know a little about the book, you may know him to be the "weeping prophet." He laments constantly over the people of Jerusalem. There's another book devoted just to his lamentations. Jeremiah is not alone in his weeping; God weeps. Yes, God is angry with their callous rejection, their continual adultery, their disgusting idolatry because God feels.

I don't know if you have thought of God as a cold and stoic judge. Passing sentence, smiting the damned, and giving them no more thought. Maybe this cold, unfeeling picture starts with our dads. Dad is our first introduction to the heavenly Father after all. If dad never expresses love or tenderness, seldom any joy, but appears only to discipline with fire in his eyes, well, we might just begin to think of God the same way.

Read this passage from Jeremiah fourteen. These are words the prophet is to speak. They sound like something he would say but notice these are God's words. This is how God feels.

"Tell these people this, Jeremiah: 'My eyes overflow with tears day and night without ceasing. For my people, my dear children, have suffered a crushing blow.

They have suffered a serious wound. If I go out into the countryside, I see those who have been killed in battle. If I go into the city, I see those who are sick because of starvation. For both prophet and priest go about their own business in the land without having any real understanding'" (Jer 14:17-18 NET).

How I Feel

Last week I shared a passage from the book of Jeremiah where the Lord revealed his own broken and hurt heart to His people. This week I want to go to the following chapter of Jeremiah where the prophet shares his own raw, unfiltered feelings about God. I say unfiltered because he even accuses God of lying to him. "Wilt thou be altogether unto me as a liar" (Jer 15:18 KJV)?

Jeremiah is so beaten down that he wishes he was never born (v 10). Everyone hates him; some have even tried to kill him. Still, he was happy to do God's work, he filled himself with God's word and it was a delight (v 15-18). As long as he had God by his side, just him and the Lord, he felt he could press on. But in this moment (or maybe more than a moment), in this season Jeremiah felt God absent. Can you empathize with him? Have you felt your need for God so acutely, heaven's support was so crucial, yet you felt so alone? You looked for God. You thought you saw Him, but the refreshment you longed for vanished like a mirage. Have you felt that?

Emotions are not to be suppressed or ignored. I think it is so valuable that we have examples of men in Scriptures, genuine heroes of faith, like Job, Elijah, and David, along with Jeremiah, who all express feelings of loneliness and disappointment, discouragement and frustration with themselves, their lot in life, and the people around them. Can I dare to say it... sometimes even with God? These are not weak men. Their faith is not less than yours. They are giants. They're honest and honest with their feelings. They hurt and when they do they take it, even when it's about God, straight to God. Sometimes they overstep. Jeremiah does as Job did, but here is something I see. God is big enough, strong enough, His shoulders are broad enough to hear about our feelings. His ego is not so fragile that we must tiptoe around His own feelings. It's uncomfortable to be with people when they are hurting. Like Job's friends, we want them to just mouth polite words or shut up. God lets them speak.

Finally, God has given us the capacity to feel, and to feel deeply both joys and sorrows, but remember this - our feelings must always be subjected and checked by truth. It's an important fact many of us need to store away: just because I feel it, doesn't make it so. Jeremiah felt alone, felt God had deceived him, but it wasn't true.

As it's typical for people, we tend to go to one extreme or the other. Some shove their feelings down, suppress them, stiffen their lip, presenting stoicism as the face of spiritual strength. Others give free range to their emotions, imagining that whatever feels right to them in the moment must be okay with God. Both have missed the heart and truth of Scripture.

Bad Sermons

Did you know that even good preachers have bad sermons? Maybe an illustration just doesn't connect with the congregation as he expected it would. Maybe the subject matter, the topic, or specific text isn't as interesting or doesn't resonate with anyone else as it does with the preacher himself.

I've had a few bad sermons over the years. Maybe more than a few... depending on who you ask. I don't remember the sermon title or anything about the subject, but I found a note this week about a Sunday morning message I gave ten years ago. I wrote, "Yesterday's sermon wasn't just bad; it was awful. I stumbled and stuttered over my words. I made the simplest points so complicated that at one point as I was speaking, I actually thought to myself, 'I don't even understand what I'm listening to.'"

Have you endured that kind of sermon? Again, I think most preachers would admit to their fair share of bellyflops from the pulpit. I've sometimes thought of the vast number of bad sermons that must have been preached over the centuries from the time of the apostles to this day. I think about it because despite those countless bad sermons, the gospel still reached the hearts of men and women. God is more than able. God can take our weak and lame efforts and do life changing things with them.

We never heard the apostle Paul speak, but it seems some felt he delivered bad sermons (2 Cor 10:10). Even if that was a fair description of his speaking ability, he wrote this about the gospel's triumphant power. "But we have this treasure in earthen vessels, that the surpassing greatness of the power may be of God and not from ourselves" (2 Cor 4:7). "And He has said to me, 'My grace is sufficient for you, for power is perfected in weakness.' Most gladly, therefore, I will rather boast about my weaknesses, that the power of Christ may dwell in me" (2 Cor 12:9).

The power to save has never been in a preacher's ability to entertain or impress. The gospel of Jesus Christ in its divine simplicity and eternal truth is what saves. That's good news for preachers like me who sometimes just don't hit it out of the park. It's good news for everyone seeking the truth, too - the weaknesses of other men cannot keep you from coming to know God.

Well, That's Not Smart

Do you spend much time reading the book of Proverbs? There are thirty-one chapters so it's convenient to read through the book every month. King Solomon sets out the purpose of reading the proverbs in chapter one. He says it is, "to learn wisdom and moral instruction, and to discern wise counsel. To receive moral instruction in skillful living, in righteousness, justice, and equity. To impart shrewdness to the morally naive, and a discerning plan to the young person" (Pr 1:2-4 NET).

Woven alongside this good advice are also all too common ways to make a mess of your life. Dads and grandpas sometimes give advice this way: "Don't spit in the wind...Try it and find out...Well, that wasn't so smart now, was it?" Here are a few from the Proverbs.

"The way of a fool is right in his own opinion" (Pr 12:15). It takes a special kind of stupid to think you are always the smartest person in the room, or that no one has any insight that might be helpful to you. Of course, we all see how ridiculous this is coming from a young know-it-all, but I think this inflated self is particularly dangerous to those of us who preach and teach. In writing about the distrust some have of commentaries, Charles Spurgeon said, "It seems odd, that certain men who talk so much of what the Holy Spirit reveals to themselves, should think so little of what

He has revealed to others." Like the Scriptures say, "with numerous advisors there is victory" (Pr 24:6). "It is an honor for a person to cease from strife, but every fool quarrels" (Pr 20:3). No matter what you say, there is some fool who will disagree just because he is disagreeable. There are so many things that just are not worth arguing about. Does it really matter which way the toilet paper rolls off the dispenser? Are you arguing, getting heated and angry because it matters or because you want to win? What a complete waste of time and energy.

"A fool rejects his father's discipline" (Pr 15:5). Thinking dad and mom are dumb, well, that's just not smart. True, dad and mom are not always right. They discipline us as seems best to them at the time (Heb 12:10), but they don't have all the answers. I'm a middle-aged man, I've lived long enough to see the weaknesses in the advice play out that older men gave me in my younger years. Still, I do not think those men were dumb, in fact, poor advice was a rare exception in their many words. It's just not smart to go around as if the older generation has nothing of value to teach. King Solomon leaves this harrowing warning later in Proverbs, "The eye that mocks at a father and despises obeying a mother—the ravens of the valley will peck it out and the young vultures will eat it" (Pr 30:17).

Recognize the Voice of God

Grandpa drove an old Chevy square body pickup. Locked in four-wheel drive he would head out to the pasture. As the sound of the old truck echoed down the hollow, grandpa's cattle would come lowing up toward him. They knew the sound of grandpa. They knew the one who brought them feed and water and salt licks.

God cared and provided for Israel from before they were even a nation. He made them numerous, gathered them up, and saved them from their oppressors. God gave them a home and blessed them in a land flowing with milk and honey. Everything they could have needed He gave to them, but they were not thankful. They forgot Him repeatedly and wondered off.

In the prophet Isaiah, God says, "An ox knows its owner, and a donkey its master's manger, but Israel does not know, My people do not understand" (Isa 1:3).

If a dumb animal knows a familiar voice, how can people not recognize the voice of God?

Jesus uses this same imagery. He explained, "My sheep hear My voice, and I know them, and they follow Me" (Jn 10:27). Now, it's true that disciples will obey or follow Jesus' instruction, just as a sheep follows its shepherd. I want to think, however, a little more about the first part of the verse - the part that is similar to the verse in Isaiah. In both, the animals recognize the voice, maybe even the presence of the provider. Could it be that people stray from God because they have forgotten He is the source of all their life's blessings? Could it be they do not recognize His voice because they have ignored His blessings in their lives?

James wrote, "Every good thing given, and every perfect gift is from above, coming down from the Father of lights, with whom there is no variation or shifting shadow" (Jas 1:17). Other writers add to this. Peter wrote, "His divine power has granted to us everything pertaining to life and godliness," (2 Pet 1:3). And Paul said to an assembly of unbelievers, "in Him we live and move and exist" (Acts 17:28).

The point I wish to make is simply this: it is all of God. Whatever good we enjoy, to whatever extent, it is the Lord's blessing. And for all these we ought to remember Him and be thankful.

"Going to church and riding horses."

His grandson summed up a childhood full of memories with this statement: "Going to church and riding horses." I spent an hour this morning at a funeral for an old farmer. He was a few years older than my own grandpa. And like my grandpa, he was a fixture of the church where they both worshipped. His family reminisced. Laughing some, crying too. It's a simple fact that no man who is driven for instant gratification can succeed as a farmer. He puts in the crop and trusts that he will harvest it later. He may work through the night, as his grandson shared, helping his mare drop her foal only for it to die. After he dries his eyes, he is heard saying, "maybe next year." A farmer is steady, patient, humble. "He didn't have to spend money to impress."

I'm so glad to live in this rural part of Illinois again for a few years and know again the men I watched as a boy. This prairie was cultivated by men - men who loved their wives and loved God. Men with calloused hands who raised crops and kids. Men who now reap a storehouse of gratitude. I think of these men, and I'm inspired to keep sowing those virtues on the hearts of my children.

Practical Discipleship

"Go, therefore, and make disciples" (Matt 28:19). Okay, but how? If you are familiar with this passage, you'll remember that Jesus continues by saying, "baptizing them."

So, we've made a disciple when we baptize a person?

Well, yes and not quite. Take, for example, a student. Disciples are often compared to learners. Are you a student when you show up for the first day of kindergarten? Yes. I remember my first day. Mom sent me to our little country schoolhouse with a Donald Duck tote bag. Maybe backpacks hadn't been invented yet, but yeah, it was a tote bag. Back to the point. No one would deny that a kindergartener is a student, but being a student goes far beyond coloring, shapes, and enjoying snacks in the afternoon.

When we think about discipleship, obviously it involves baptism. Maybe you have a few lessons that you like to walk people through - a home study on Biblical authority. Another lesson on the nature of the church and another on scriptural worship. Maybe there's a final study on God's plan of salvation leading to baptism. That's fine. Something like that I think is needed, but what about after? If they accept and are baptized, what then? What if, on the other hand, they don't want to be baptized? Is it a lost cause after just four or five lessons?

At the end of Philippians, Paul gives a concise picture of discipleship. He writes, "The things you have learned and received and heard and seen in me, practice these things" (Phil 4:9).

God entrusted a son to me. I see my job as his dad to be one of discipling - discipling him in manhood. Sometimes he gets lectures, i.e., the "dad talk", every now and then. Sometimes I give him jobs and chores to do, tasks that as dads say, "build character". But I suspect that most of my discipling him in manhood is done when he watches me. He sees what I do. He's not taking notes. I'd guess he doesn't even know he is learning anything, but he is, and a day will come when he is in some situation and the examples he witnessed will find their value.

Something to remember about discipleship is that it takes a long time... much more than a few weeks. Invest, then, in practical discipleship. Yes, preach the word, give the lectures that are needed, have the home studies, but let people see you living the life of a disciple. Model the behavior for them.

Most of us realize that we only start to have a good fix on parenting when our children are nearly grown. There are plenty of books about parenting. You can argue about which fad author has the best ideas. Mine are simple. Practical. Be an adult. Model the behavior you want your children to develop. Discipling Christians is the same. Be a Christian. Live it.

Knowing Christ

"In view of the surpassing value of knowing Christ Jesus my Lord...I have suffered the loss of all things and count them but rubbish so that I may gain Christ" (Phil 3:8).

It's typical for Americans to want a bigger house, more rooms, more space. My house seems far too big for just my son and me. We basically live in just one room. We could probably get by in a camper, but I don't think I'm immune to materialism and wants. I'd love a three-car garage. I could get another project car, and then more tools, and maybe some outdoor toys. I sure miss my brother-in-law living just a street over from us; he had such a great shop in the backyard. My kids spent many nights in auto shop at the homeschool annex, otherwise known as Uncle James' house. Maybe my son, on the other hand, wants a faster computer. If we both got what we wanted, we'd both go off to our solitary corners day after day. Eventually he'd move out. We would still recognize one another's faces, but hardly know each other. Have you seen families at restaurants, gathered round the same table, but each secluded to the bubble of their own smart phone? "Memories are made around the table" was a saying on the wall of my mom's dining room. How very true. Houses, computers, smart phones are all blessings. They can be used to build relationships, but they can also hinder families from knowing one another.

Do you suppose there are blessings in our lives that we are misusing and are now keeping us from knowing Christ fully?

Go Ahead and Tell Them

I've always wanted a Mustang. Well, that's a bit of a stretch. I've always wanted a cool project car... actually, a truck. One of those old ones with a three speed on the steering column. Yeah, that's more my style. But a few summers back, I saw an ad for a Mustang. Late '90s model, V8, five speed manual, and for added coolness, a convertible. It needed some serious engine work, but this would be perfect. My son and I could work on it together in the garage. We'd fix it up and have so much fun doing it.

My son wasn't so passionate about it. Like a stereotypical dad, I never bothered to ask if working on a car in the sweltering garage would be something he'd like, I just assumed he would. I was left doing most of it myself, but occasionally one of my girls would stroll out to the garage and tinker on it a little with me.

The engine was nearly back together when one of my daughters came out to watch one afternoon, but I was getting frustrated. A bolt in one of those hard-to-reach places and harder still to get a wrench on was needing to be addressed. I'd get close and then drop the wrench. Stop, crawl under the car to look for it, get back up, maneuver awkwardly back into position to tighten the bolt down. Clank. Again, down goes the wrench through the engine bay. And for good measure, I probably smashed my knuckles too. I don't remember how many times this cycle repeated, but this time I looked across the car to my girl and said, "Megan, if I drop it again, we are going inside."

That night I thought about it. What had I taught her? What had she learned from me? This was more than learning a bit about cars. There were life lessons I'd hoped to share with the kids. I thought my message was that if you are frustrated it is better to take a break than let fly with your anger and break something. I thought that was what I was modeling for her, but thinking about it, she could have got the message that if something is hard, just quit.

She could have taken either message from that day. How could I make sure she understood the one I wanted to teach. Well first, we did finish tightening the bolt eventually and took the car around for a drive. But additionally, I just went ahead and told her what I was trying to model.

I want to set a good example. I want to let my light shine in my home and in the world. "A picture is worth a thousand words." "I'd rather see a sermon than hear one." Someone said that. They put it into words. They didn't convey the message with just a picture. I don't want my practice to be contrary to my preaching, but with the important things, it's best to spell them out. Just go ahead and tell them.

Conversations With God

"It happened that while Jesus was praying in a certain place, after He had finished, one of His disciples said to Him, 'Lord, teach us to pray just as John also taught his disciples'" (Lk 11:1).

There are many things we can learn from books. When I began homeschooling my children, my older sister encouraged me by saying, "if you can only teach them to read and do basic math, they will be okay." Not that this would be the goal of a good education, but being able to read provides a tool to go and learn from a book what they might later need to know. Yes, there are plenty of things that you can learn this way, but there are a few things we learn best by being shown.

I want to sketch an image of prayer. Conversational prayer. Talking with God. Half a mile from my house is our local village park. A half mile paved roadencircles it. In the years that I have lived here in Palestine, I have worn out shoes on that blacktop path. It's where I walk several miles a day. When my daughters still lived at home with me and after finishing schoolwork, we would all head out to the park. We didn't all walk at the same pace and some preferred to ride a bike, but more than a few times I might jog up to one of them and we would walk awhile together. As we walked side by side, we would chat. Occasionally, they might share some heavy weight on their heart with me. Sometimes they would just talk about the nice day or what they would like to do that evening. And sometimes they might not say anything at all; we would just walk together.

What does our talking to God look like? Does it have to begin with "dear heavenly father", conclude with "in Jesus' name Amen", and have a continuous stream of confessions and wants and worries in between? Could prayer be compared to a boy or girl talking with their dad?

Just like my children often spoke with me at the park, I do much of my praying there too. Sometimes I confess fears and my worries over the future. Sometimes I tell God what I have enjoyed about the morning. I know He has brought the breeze that refreshes me and the peaceful nature of my small-town life that has restored my exhausted spirit. Sometimes I tell God about people who are on my mind or the work I'm doing. Sometimes I have serious things to tell God. Sometimes it's light conversation. Sometimes one flows into the other. And sometimes, I don't say much. We simply walk together in the cool of the day.

How Long Will It Last?

We are back to our expository study of Luke this morning. I find this sort of preaching so helpful. It's powerful, life changing, and it keeps both the Scriptures and preacher in their proper place. God's power to save is in the gospel preached not the gospel preacher. I simply want to hold up God's message in its purity and let it have the effect God intends it to produce.

Reading and meditating on a few chapters in Luke, seeing how he weaves Jesus' story together, Luke's intended point becomes clear. It's a far more powerful and impressive sermon than any motivational speaker could craft. Here are a few principles in the account of Jesus casting out the legion of devils (Lk 8:26-39).

First, I see some irony in this scary man being scared of Jesus, and even more so, the town's people are scared of Jesus. Luke describes the possessed man as a frightening figure. Wouldn't you be skittish of a naked man who runs around shouting and screaming? You'd stay as far away from him as you possibly could. He's toxic. I think of Pigpen in the Charlie Brown cartoons. Everywhere he goes, the cloud of filth perpetually radiates off him. So it is with those enslaved by the devil.

Second, Jesus and Jesus alone healed this destructive and dangerous man. I want to be careful in how I phrase this. I have several self-help books that are helpful. I have been to counseling to address some of my own personal challenges. As a gospel minister, I've coached people in the Christian walk and have received that coaching from others too. I fully recognize that there are steps to crucifying the old man and putting on the new. I am ashamed to admit it, however, that the one action that would help the most is the one I've given so much lip service to but neglected. Only in this past year did the weight of it finally connect. I openly confess that I am a broken man with very deep hurts. I have plastered over the scars with good behavior, but the wounds still fester underneath, and sometimes infection has leaked out. It's hurtful to myself and those around me. Like that demon possessed man, there are not chains strong enough to make me good. No rules to make me whole. I'm just a man naked and crying out before God while living among the dead. Lord, if I am ever going to be healed, You must heal me.

Last, if we rely simply on rules to keep sinners inline, and the heart is not renewed, how long before those chains break? A danger for the town was that while the man was now sitting, clothed and reasonable, how long would it last? It's safer for everyone to be cautiously optimistic. Here again is a problem for the "rules only" approach to Christianity. It fosters a judgmental skepticism among brethren.

I Just Don't Feel Like It

It's Sunday morning. Are you up? Are you dressed and ready for worship? Are you going today? Long ago, before Jesus built His church, back when God's people worshiped Him in a tent, David said, "I was glad when they said to me, 'Let us go to the house of the Lord'" (Psalms 122:1). Could you express the same feelings this morning? It's time for worship... are you glad?

Christians enjoy worship. They enjoy the fellowship with God's children and singing His praises together. They find comfort speaking to Him in prayer with thanksgiving, and they are glad for His counsel revealed through the study of Scripture. Yes, Christians enjoy worship. That is - they enjoy worship most of the time.

Have you ever woken up on Sunday morning and just not felt like going to worship? I'm not talking about being ill but just not motivated. A midweek Bible study approaches and you just don't feel like showing up? Would you think I am a bad Christian and an even worse preacher if I confessed right now that I have?

I know preachers are the guys who try to encourage and lift other people's spirits. They're supposed to be positive and upbeat, the church cheerleader. Those are more assumptions than specific job descriptions. Still, preachers, preacher's wives, deacons, elders, and all Christians should encourage others because they themselves are encouraging. To tell you the truth, however, sometimes I am just down. Demoralized like Elijah (1 Kings 19:10). Exhausted like the Lord Jesus (Jn 4:6). Mentally fatigued like the apostle Paul (2 Cor 4:8; 11:28). Now if you have ever felt like that or even feel somewhat like that today, maybe you'll let me offer you this one suggestion - go anyway.

I know some may say: "But if my heart isn't in it and I just go through the motions, I will feel like a hypocrite." You're wrong about that. Listen, a hypocrite is a person that condemns in others what they excuse in themselves. The hypocrite tells other people to go while they stay home inventing excuses for themselves.

It's Sunday morning. It's time for worship. Let's get up and go. Go today even if you don't feel like it because once you're there your feelings may change, and besides, sometimes the things we want to do the least are precisely what we need to do the most.

I hope to see you today. Let's encourage each other.

Cancel Culture

"You can't say that!" That's being said all the time. I know you know what I'm talking about. I'm sure you can at least think of a few examples of no-no words, or opinions that will get you quickly labeled as racist, sexist, homophobic, transphobic, xenophobic, misogynistic, legalistic, or a science denier. Hold on, let me get on Twitter quickly... I'm sure there are half a dozen more labels being fired off to shame, silence, shut down, and intimidate.

This is nothing new. Those with power never want their position challenged. After Jesus' resurrection, Peter and John were arrested for telling people that He was alive. Those in power threatened them, "commanded them not to speak or teach at all in the name of Jesus" (Ac 4:18). Stephen was called a blasphemer. He was shouted down as the Jewish leaders gnashed their teeth at him and finally murdered him with the weapons of Cain, who likewise killed his own brother (Ac 7:54, 58).

No, this cancel culture is nothing new. Reading through the prophet Jeremiah, this same violent intent was aimed at his words. Men from a certain city plotted to kill Jeremiah. "They warn, 'do not prophesy in the name of the Lord, or you will certainly die at our hand'" (Jer. 11:21).

When God called Jeremiah in the beginning of the book He told him, "Now, get ready. Stand up and tell them everything that I commanded you. Do not be intimidated by them or I will cause you to cower before them...They will fight against you but never prevail over you, since I am with you to rescue you" (Jer. 1:17,19). We must keep speaking truth. Truth about gender - there are only two. God made them male and female (Gen 1:27). Truth about marriage - loving leadership is not toxic and voluntary submission is not slavery (Eph 5:22, 25). Truth about sexuality - sleeping around is not empowering to women. Pornography is not victimless. Sex outside of marriage is sin as is all homosexuality, "for fornicators and adulterers God will judge" (Heb 13:4).

Will you get canceled for saying these things? Likely not from the people reading this bulletin. But do not fool yourself, the god of this world will certainly exact a price for your convictions. Speak the truth. "But they won't listen," you say. It doesn't matter. Truth must have a voice. Again, you say, "But even my family thinks I am a bigot now." Yes, that's a high price, but you're in good company, "in the same way they persecuted the prophets who were before you" (Matt 5:12).

Stop Praying

Is there ever a time to stop praying? Jesus tells the story of the unrighteous judge to encourage us to always pray and not lose heart (Lk 18:1). But maybe there is a time to stop. Maybe we shouldn't pray for some people.

"Thus says the LORD to this people, 'Even so they have loved to wander; they have not kept their feet in check. Therefore, the LORD does not accept them; now He will remember their iniquity and call their sins to account.' So, the LORD said to me, 'Do not pray for the welfare of this people'" (Jer. 14:10-11).

It sounds strange, but this is the third time that the Lord had told Jeremiah not to pray for His people (Jer. 7:16, 11:14). Doesn't this prohibition seem strange? Prayer, after all, is a godly person's native tongue. That sounds like a quote, but I don't remember where I heard the phrase. It's so true, isn't it? In good times and bad, a godly person's first words are always prayer. So, it was with Jeremiah. In verses two through nine the prophet petitions the Lord. So why would God now forbid this righteous man from praying further?

Here is another similar passage that gives some insight. "If anyone sees his brother committing a sin not leading to death, he shall ask and God will for him give life to those who commit sin not leading to death. There is a sin leading to death; I do not say that he should make request for this" (1 Jn 5:16). The Bible clearly states that all sin ends in death (Gen 2:17; Rom 6:23; Jas 1:15). But John said there was a sin that doesn't. Some do and some don't... so how are we to know the difference between them?

Look back to what God tells Jeremiah. The prophet asked, "Why art Thou like a stranger in the land or like a traveler who has pitched his tent for the night" (Jer 14:8)? God informs Jeremiah that he has this backwards. It is the people who love to wander.

They are the ones who are like a traveler. They stop in to see the Lord, but after a short visit, they are anxious to get back on the road to idolatry and make up for lost time. The people are intent to live in sin and so God tells Jeremiah not to intercede for them. In John's letter, God's point is the same. A sin that leads to death is any sin from which a person refuses to repent. To then pray that God forgive these callous and unrepentant people anyway would be against God's will (1 Jn 5:14-15). We shouldn't expect requests like these to be granted.

What do you think – in the case of these rebellious people, is it appropriate to pray that God bring circumstances into their lives, even hardships, that would lead them to repentance?

Enjoy Your Life

Ecclesiastes is one of the wisdom books of Scripture. In it Solomon employs his vast wisdom and insight to seek out and find lasting happiness. However, the thing about happiness is that you never find it by looking for it or catch it by chasing it. This is borne out in Solomon's conclusions. Some misunderstand his point and see only despair in his commentary on life. Focusing predominantly on the line, "Vanity of vanities! All is vanity...I have seen all the works which have been done under the sun, and behold, all is vanity and striving after wind (Eccl 1:2, 14). This pessimism, however, is not Solomon's intent. Consider what he encourages people to do in a later chapter.

"Go then, eat your bread in happiness, and drink your wine with a cheerful heart; for God has already approved your works. Let your clothes be white all the time and let not oil be lacking on your head. Enjoy life with the woman whom you love all the days of your fleeting life which He has given to you under the sun; for this is your reward in life, and in your toil in which you have labored under the sun. Whatever your hand finds to do, verily, do itwith all your might; for there is no activity or planning or knowledge or wisdom in Sheol where you are going" (Eccl 9:7-10).

In previous verses, Solomon has explained that everyone will eventually pass from this life. We all know it's true, and when we pass, all our pursuits and dreams, our ambitions and hopes, all cease. Solomon's point, therefore, is that we ought to enjoy our life while we are living.

I have an afghan my mother crocheted before she went to be with the Lord. Some have said I should put it away and keep it safe... I'll never get another after all. But, it was made to be used. Besides, if I were to fold it up and store it away in a chest for years, what then? My children will sort through my belongings someday. They may find it and use it but without understanding the special meaning it has to me.Worse, they might donate it and some stranger would take it and throw it to his dog for a bed.

"Eat, drink, and be merry." It's a familiar phrase and the thought is not lost on Solomon. We can peel away our days, saving for tomorrow, until not a single day is left. Then all that we have sacrificed will be for what? There is value in saving because we do not know what tomorrow has in store. For the same reason, however,we should not entirely pass over opportunities to enjoy the fruit of our labors today.

I was Too Proud to Take It Then...
Now I Can't Give It Back

Tony, my youngest brother, shared something mom said to him years ago. My brother Kevin and I were renting a place together in Indianapolis. He was in school and I was working nights. We had come home for a visit and later when we got ready to leave, mom made a care package for us. We snuck out without taking it. We were grown men, after all, not babies. We didn't need our mom to take care of us anymore. I wanted her to be proud of me, to see she raised us to be self-sufficient. I'm sure she was proud of us, but my youngest brother told me that when we left mom said to him, "don't be like your brothers when you leave home, take what I give you." I never knew she said that until a few weeks ago when he mentioned it.

I've been thinking about that. Thinking about her. What a beautiful soul! She never went to college or had an exciting career, but she was wiser than most, frugal, and resourceful. She gave birth to six children, buried one and raised five. She helped raise other children too; the ones she watched during the day to help provide some income for the family. They loved her so much that some drove a good distance to pay their respects at her funeral. It's hard to believe,but she was married and nursing a baby when she was the age that my two baby girls are today. I don't know what her teenage dreams may have been, but I know what she was - she was a wonderful mother. She is worthy of a monument even if built only of memories. When dad and I were getting up for work before daylight, mom would get up with us to make us breakfast and pack us lunch. She may have gone back to bed after we left for the day, but she always got up with us. I so wish I could sit down at her table or just unwrap a plain bologna sandwich that her hands had prepared. I wish I could give back to her what I took that day I left without her care package in hand. Now, no number of flowers can make up for it. I'm sure she forgave me even right then. I just didn't understand. Giving people can only be giving if someone is willing to receive.

What Has Christ Cost Me?

"I count all things to be loss in view of the surpassing value of knowing Christ Jesus my Lord, for whom I have suffered the loss of all things" (Phil 3:8). Paul mentions that he has given up many things for Christ's sake, but he's not talking about casting off sinful behaviors and desires. Christians must, of course, consider their bodies to be dead to all that is sinful (Col 3:5). But more, Paul has given up hopes and ambitions, status, and likely, lifelong friends as well as colleagues.

I know there are Christians who have followed Paul's brave example. Many have left behind their family's religious tradition and with it, sometimes family. I remember reading several articles some years ago by preachers addressing "Why I Left" a particular denomination. I find it difficult, however, to identify with Paul in this. Fellowship with Jesus seemingly hasn't cost me much. I grew up around church people. My parents were Christians; my dad was even a preacher himself for part of my childhood. Grandparents, uncles and aunts, cousins - almost all are members of the church. Even most of my friends have been Christians both when I was young and to this very day. When I was baptized a lot about my life did not change.

Taking a note from those old articles by brethren who left various denominations, I'd like to ask you a question. Especially, I want to pose this to churchgoers such as myself, who grew up in the church as we sometimes say... why did you stay?

While following Christ did not cost me as much as it has other Christians at the outset, leaving apathy, pushing beyond the status quo, and making the Faith my faith was not easy. Truthfully, the cost of maintaining my walk with Christ now after many years of being a Christian is much higher than I would have at first imagined.

The Weaker Vessel

Last month I was blessed with the opportunity to hear a series of sermons dedicated to family. The first lesson was entitledThe Husband Your Wife Needs. The second was the other side - The Wife Your Husband Needs. I missed the last lesson about the responsibility and value of grandparents.

Naturally, 1 Peter 3:7 will come up when thinking about what God says to husbands and wives. "Likewise, ye husbands, dwell with them according to knowledge, giving honor unto the wife, as unto the weaker vessel, and as being heirs together of the grace of life; that your prayers be not hindered." It's amazing how much push back this verse gets, even from Christians. The feminist chant of "I'm a strong, independent woman who doesn't need a man" has filtered into the church. And no wonder... little girls and boys have been taught that anything a boy can do, girls can do better. This fostering of competition rather than complement is and will be ruinous.

Now, I do not like the way modern translations phrase this verse. "As with someone weaker" (NASB); "The weaker partner" (NIV); The weaker sex (NRSV). These are all interpretations more than translations. Yet what is meant by weaker? It's not a slight to women, but instruction to husbands.

Let me share an illustration with you. Last month I fractured a rib mountain biking in Brown County, Indiana. Well, it wasn't the biking part so much as the fast and spectacular dismount that caused the problem. I finished the day with some cuts on one leg and a few more souvenirs on the other - no big deal. Walk it off, you'll be fine. But these fragile, tender bones under my arm... that's no joke! I never thought a lot about it, but do you realize how much a person's ribs affect every little thing they do? Why would you think about it when everything is fine? But oh, it hurts! It hurts just to breath. It hurts to stand up, to bend over, to tie my shoes. And listen, one time I sneezed, and my vision went dark. I promised never to do that again.

Paul says, "no one ever hated his own flesh, but nourishes and cherishes it" (Eph 5:29). In the same way, men ought to treat their wives. I have been extra careful now about how I get up in the morning. I've had to put off some of my regular routine or change other parts of it. I've been extra gentle with every movement, and I promise I have done everything in my power to avoid any risk of ever sneezing again.

I want my body to heal, and it will. Just give it time and what it needs. I'd be a fool though to keep pushing, to push through the pain.

Do you suppose it is more than a little significant that God made woman from the side of man? Like the rib from which she was formed, a man's wife affects every part of his life. Should he not treat her with extra special care?

You Cannot be Replaced

In our Sunday Bible study, we were thinking about being members of one anotheras the body of Christ and a person's body is one but composed of many individual members all serving various purposes. The Bible illustrates this saying, "if the whole body were an eye, where would the hearing be..." (1 Cor 12:17). Some church members will say, "what can I do though, what purpose do I serve, what can I contribute?"

Someone in the Bible study mentioned their grandpa. In his later years he couldn't work the farm as hard as before. They still let him do little things even though they could have done the jobs faster without him. They wanted him to feel needed. Take a man's job away and many times his reason for living goes too.

Many in the church feel they have nothing to contribute. If they cannot preach or lead the worship in some manner, what can they do? So, we spent a few minutes thinking up some little jobs we are all glad someone does. "Somebody always makes sure the toilet paper is replaced in the restroom. We are all glad for that, right?"

I'm still thinking of the brother's grandpa piddling on the farm. Piddling is what my grandpa would have called it. Is it our job to sooth his ego by scrounging up some odd job for him? "See, grandpa, you're still needed." Everything he does someone else could do faster and even better. When he is gone, someone else will. His contribution can be replaced easily but not the man. No one can replace grandpa. And no one can replace you.

The Nations Rage

You've heard the news. You can't hardly hide from it. Completely ignoring it won't make it go away either. World leaders are beating their chests and flexing their muscles. The nations are raging. Armies are moving and we do not know how the world will look when the huffing and puffing has tired itself out.

Isaiah spoke long before Vladimir Putin, Xi Jinping, or Joe Biden murmured their first word (or whoever the blowhards are when you are reading this.) Long before the empires over which they rule had any influence in the world, Isaiah spoke of other nations and leaders just as loud, just as dangerous, and this is what he said, "Ah! The roar of many peoples — they roar like the roaring of the seas. The raging of the nations — they rage like the rumble of rushing water. The nations rage like the rumble of a huge torrent. He rebukes them, and they flee far away, driven before the wind like chaff on the hills and like tumbleweeds before the gale. In the evening — sudden terror! Before morning — it is gone! This is the fate of those who plunder us and the lot of those who ravage us" (Isa 17:12-14).

I pray never to know the sound of war or invasion as those in Ukraine heard this week, but I'm sure Isaiah's imagery of a flash flood or the crash of the incoming tide is accurate. Don't minimize the threat. It's frightening. The strength of the current is no joke and neither are the weapons of war. I cannot help, however, when reading this passage in Isaiah to think of Jesus soundly sleeping while the sea waves raged. In the evening, there was sudden terror. His disciples feared for their very lives, but by morning, the fearsome waves were gone. Jesus was in control.

I do not know how to solve the issues of the world. I know that people who lust for power willingly sacrifice their own young men chasing it. I know, too, that others will sacrifice more blood to hold onto the influence they already have. People are no different today than they always were. But I also know God is still in control even if He appears, like Jesus, to be sleeping. The Lord is in heaven, on the throne in His holy temple, right where He belongs (Hab 2:20).

When Evil Is Rewarded

"If a ruler listens to lies, all his officials will be wicked" (Pr 29:12 CSB). Many of the proverbs of the Bible, especially in this chapter, deal with leaders and kings. The lasting power of these wise sayings, however, is in their wide application. You don't need to be a king or a powerful figure in the world to find an appropriate place for these words in your life.

The simple meaning of the proverb is that you will get more of what you reward. Understanding this can create great momentum in a company. For example, with sales, the better you perform, the more you will make. But the opposite is also true just as the proverb takes a negative perspective. Some parents fumble this proverb though they don't intend to. If you ignore your child except when they misbehave, don't be surprised when your child continues to act out. You've rewarded the wrong behavior.

Culturally speaking it shouldn't be a shock that our social fabric is worn out. Women will sleep with a string of uncommitted men and so men are uninterested in commitment. The trashiest behavior on TikTok is rewarded with fame and popularity. Coming out as bi, poly, and trans is cheered with social credit. Mass shooters are immortalized in the media with their names and faces continuously repeated.

"Why does this keep happening?" What a dumb question. It happens because it works; it's what's being rewarded.

Finish Well

I know today is Christmas and because it happens to also fall on a Sunday, it would be extra convenient to say something about the birth of Jesus and Christians celebrating various holidays. But I'll leave that to other preachers today. Today also happens to be the last Sunday of this year and that's what I'd like to highlight for your devotional thinking.

There is one more week in this year to do God's work, to serve one another, to reflect Jesus' holiness into the world. There is just one more week, so finish well.

I know many of us will be sleeping off the overindulgence of cookies and sweets - all the rich food we will enjoy with family this coming week. From Thanksgiving until now, our lives haven't run on neat schedules, as they do most of the year. We just try to hang on and get through New Year's, then we can get back to "normal" and even make a resolution to do a little better. How about this - finish this year well.

A few years ago, my children and I along with my brother and my niece, participated in the local Turkey Trot. It's a five-kilometer race on Thanksgiving Day morning. FiveKs are lots of fun. It's just a few steps past three miles. Everybody's positive and encouraging. You even get a shirt and a banana at the end. I've encouraged friends to do these little runs, but the answers are often, "I don't think I can run three miles." That's okay; you can walk the whole thing. I've done far longer runs than a 5K and guess what - I've walked a bit in each of them. You can stumble. You can fall. You can spill Gatorade all over your face. Learning to drink from a dixie cup while running takes some practice. Whatever happens though, when you see the end in sight, run. Even if you have walked the whole distance. We walked the entire Turkey Trot, but at the end, we all ran across the finish line. That's finishing well.

Today is the last Sunday of the year. Maybe your church attendance has been sporadic this year. Maybe it's been more than a year since the last time you went to church. Whatever it has been, go today. Meet with His people and worship, sing praises and offer prayers with thanksgiving because He is gracious. Finish well.

This is the last week of the year, only six more days. Even if you haven't yet begun a daily Bible reading program, make time to listen to God this week. Read a few chapters the next six days. Finish well.

The end of this year is in sight. Have you shared the hope and forgiveness Jesus brings? Have you sown even a single seed for the kingdom? Maybe over past months you have tarnished your Christian example. Maybe rather than pointing people to God, you have discouraged them, soured them on Christianity. Whatever it was yesterday, why wait until New Year's? The finish line is in sight. Run. Finish well.

Habits For the New Year

JANUARY 1, 2023

A lot of us are thinking today of making a good start for the year as we often do around New Year's Day. I want to start out well myself and have compiled a list of habits to form or focus on in the months ahead.

I want to nourish my spirit with Scripture. Does your stomach ever rumble? Have you ever been hangry? Yes, it's a real thing. For me, Reese's peanut butter cups will stop the growling, but I usually feel pretty awful after half a dozen. I need something more nutritious. When my spirit is famished and I'm weak, drained, and faint, I can shut down in front of the television. I can feed my spirit with junk that simply fills the empty space but it's never quite satisfying. It often leaves me in despair and depressed. I know my spirit needs God's word (Isa 61:1-2; 1 Pet 2:2).

I want to build a strong faith. In the past, I have done some running—not fast, just forward. I do basic calisthenics in the mornings. When I started exercising with friends at a gym, I was quickly humbled. I was nowhere near as fit as I thought and not even remotely close to where I'd like to be. Do you know where the change takes place - where weak muscles become strong? It's the resistance, the strain, the challenge. I want a strong faith but the only way this spiritual muscle grows is by meeting ever more challenging tests and trials. As James says, "Consider it all joy, my brethren, when you encounter various trials, knowing that the testing of your faith produces endurance" (Jas 1:2, 3).

I want to be mindful of my words. I want to speak carefully and with clarity - not only as a minister but as a Christian. I want to represent Jesus faithfully. Jesus was truth (Jn 14:6), so I want to speak the truth (Eph 4:15, 25). Jesus was gentle with people who were hurting and beatdown (Matt 9:36; 11:28), so I want to be gracious (even to people who do not deserve it.)Everyone knows an injured dog will bite, and sometimes those who are mean are themselves hurting, so I want to speak to people better than they deserve (Col 4:6).

I want to control my thoughts. Paul's letter to the Philippians focuses heavily on a Christian's mindset. Yes, he does say a lot about joy, but this joy is rooted in the mind. Get your mind right and everything else will fit into its proper place (Phil 4:8).

I want to be more fully committed to God's will. I know, and you know too, that God's will is self-denial and a cross (Matt 16:24). That cross may be forgoing my rights so I do not trip up someone else (Matt 17:24-27). It may require me to leave the comforts and stability of my present lifestyle to go out seeking the lost sheep (Matt 18:12-14). The cross may be confronting an erring Christian and possibly, it may require severing our relationship (Matt 18:15-20). That's a cross. It could be forgiving some deep hurt (Matt 18:21-35), living a lonely life (Matt 19:1-12), or it may mean impoverishment and taking a lowly, dependent station in life (Matt 19:16-26). Whatever cross the Lord has for me, I want to carry it.

Finally, whatever failures I had last year, whatever wounds I experienced, or sins I committed, I want to lay them down before Jesus (1 Pet 5:7). This year I want to let go of the baggage (Jas 1:21; 1 Cor 6:18; Heb 12:1). All those things we've been carrying are not keepsakes; they're just clutter.

Not Resolutions, But Perpetual Goals

We know how it goes, don't we?One year ends and with the start of the new, we make a list of resolutions. We mean well but we all laugh and joke about how soon the resolutions fail. Did you make it even to the second day?

It may be semantics, but I resolved some years ago to never make resolutions again. I do however make a list of goals in December. Some are taken from my bucket list... again, not a phrase that I like, but it's language everyone understands. Some of my goals are not so concrete, for example -lose twenty pounds or read one book a month. Some are more open ended. Some are not made to be checked off the list but rather checked up on periodically. So here is my never finished, perpetual list of goals.

1.	Be a good man, holy and confident. I hate the term "nice guy." Nice guys really aren't nice at all. It's often a manipulative tactic to get what they want. Rather, I want to genuinely be good, steady, respectable - all of which breeds confidence (1 Jn 4:17-18).

2.	Tell people what they mean to me. I don't want to be a blubbering mess all of the time, but I've spoken at many funerals and no-one there regrets being too free with the "I love yous." (Phil 1:7).

3.	Forgive them. It doesn't matter who they are. I want to wipe out any chance of bitterness or anger fromever again taking root in my soul. Holding a grudge causes them no hurt and only imprisons me longer.

4.	Encourage young preachers and their wives. I don't feel like an old preacher, but there are a lot of men preaching now that are younger than me. A few older brothers had a tremendousimpact on me. In whatever capacity I can, I want to do likewise for young guys. And for my sisters, I pray I'll always have a soft and encouraging word.

5.	Give someone hope/renew their faith. As a teenager, I remember standing at the opening of the hay loft after hours of heavy work. Tired. Sweating. Covered in dirt. The breeze would blow past my face. What a relief in that stifling barn! Some people came into my life for only a moment, but they blew into my soul such welcomed joy. Let me refresh someone like that (Matt 10:42; 1 For 16:18; 2 Tim 1:16).

6.	Love someone without need or want. How do I explain this? We have legitimate needs and it's perfectly healthy to want them to be met by friends, family, and partners. However, I want to give love without the expectation, especially unspoken expectations, of getting something in return.

7.   Pray to move a mountain. "When you pray that the mountain moves, in faith you pick up a shovel." I don't reject that, but I've found some temptations, some wounds, some broken pieces cannot be healed by reading another self-help book or implementing another counselor's strategy. God heals me. Only He can move this mountain (Matt 21:21).

Count Your Blessings

A demonstration may be the best instruction. When Jesus taught the disciples to pray, He prayed (Lk 11:1-4). When He taught them to serve, He served (Jn 13:1-20).

Last Sunday evening here in Robinson, I had a list of passages addressing thankfulness. It'd be easy to build a sermon on why we should be thankful, for what we should be thankful, and so on. As we read through the verses, many from Psalms and Paul's writings, it became clear that these men are not technically teaching us how to be thankful. They simply are thankful.

I want to embody this spirit of thankfulness. I want praise for God's generosity to radiate out of me. I want to be so overflowing with sincere gratitude that I cannot help it from spilling out whenever I open my mouth. With what space I have left here I'm just going to begin giving thanks.

"Father, it's a simple thing but you know how much I like it - I am thankful for my front porch and the glider swing my sister left me. It's a good place to pray, meditate, and enjoy both mornings and evenings. I'm thankful for the time to do those things too, and I know I have that time because I work as a preacher. I'm thankful to still be preaching. God, you know several times in the past I thought I was being pushed out of ministry. But you have blessed me to serve at Robinson. Even more, I thank you for the brethren here. I feel ashamed for being divorced. Whether this shame is deserved or not, I still carry it. I know I don't look like a good "mascot" for the church. I don't have a neat family image. Mine is messy, but your people here have never made me feel unfit. They all treat me with confidence and trust. I'm thankful - thankful that you can take my mess and refashion and reform it into something wonderful. This is a joy bigger than I could have hoped for at the start.

Father, I'm thankful for the past few years I've spent with my children here at home. Thankful for reading Little House books on winter afternoons and summer talks while we walked at the village park. Father, what I've sown in their lives, please, do not let it be lost.

I'm thankful all my siblings live only two hours away. I haven't always had them so close. I am especially thankful to witness how you enriched my brother's life. He has a fun and godly wife, a spirited daughter, and a little boy. Even through his health scares and their moving, I watched You work. I've seen You work in all of this and in the lives of other people too. How can I do anything other than trust Your providence even more? You do everything right and right on time.

I'm thankful for others You have brought into my life through the years. I wouldn't embarrass them by naming them here, but You know their names. Some make such good company in life. Others have only touched my life briefly, but the impact was tremendous. Thank You for each one of them. Use me in the same way. Let me be Your blessing to someone.

Thank You for this computer that I'm typing on right now. It feels unworthy to be mentioned alongside people and relationships, but it was such a big deal and I want to use it to do encouraging work. I still do not know who gave me the money to buy it. It was just waiting in an envelope on the podium for me. You know who they are.

Father, I feel like I receive from brethren here and elsewhere far more than I can give. I shovel and pile up what good I can on them, but your shovel is always bigger.

You use many hands and many shovels to pile blessing back on me. Thank you." - Amen

25 Years

I've been wearing my grandpa Brooks' wristwatch for years now. It was just an inexpensive K-Mart purchase, but I'm kind of sentimental, so it's valuable to me. Still, a better-quality watch would be nice. I told my friend, John, that I started located preaching 25 years ago this November in Olney, Illinois and that I thought I'd find a new watch for the occasion.

A box came in the mail this week. Enclosed was a watch and two notes - one from John and one from my dad. John had reached out to my dad and they put this gift together. I immediately called John after reading the notes. He asked how I liked the engraving. I hadn't even looked at the watch close enough to notice. but etched on the back is: "25 years". 2 Tim 4:1-5, Dad & John

I like it very much. Like I said, I'm sentimental about things but even more about relationships. Dad and John, I love you guys.

Thinking over my own experience through these years, along with that of other preachers and so many good brethren, let me share something more with you. The church is not a business - it's a family. I understand that there are tax issues both for the church and the preacher that we must comply with.However, do not let government labels warp your thinking. I do not see myself as an employee of the church. I am a slave of Jesus Christ and a minister to His people.

Further, the church and its elders are not employers. Again, I think we understand that money and service is being exchanged, but a business mindset has often created animosity between preachers and the congregation—the working man vs corporate. We should detest our Father's family being thought of and ran like a business. Didn't Jesus detest his Father's house being made a house of merchandise (Jn 2:16)? Can you imagine the ruined relationships this business mindset would create if we tried it in any one of our homes?

Remember in Revelation, the most lucrative church was completely failing (Rev 3:14-22), but a successful church looked like a weak and failing business (Rev 2:8-11). This is similarly true of leadership. Good business sense is not a requirement for an elder, but a poor man may be well qualified to shepherd the church. "Did not God choose the poor of this world to berich in faith" (Jas 2:5)? Yes, shepherding is work. Heavy and emotional (Heb 13:17). Preaching is too (2 Cor 11:28; 1 Thess 2:7; 2 Tim 2:3), but it's not corporate work. It's family work, relationship work. As Jesus taught, "You are all brothers" (Matt 23:8).

What I'd want to encourage fellow ministers to remember, and prayerfully what I desire to live out, is this: do not get so caught up in the profession of preaching that people take second place. I've always been treated well by brethren - local Christians I work with and distant ones who have supported me with their prayers and money. But sometimes there are dustups as it goes in relationships and families. Make every effort, though, to work through them. I'll repeat that... don't miss it. Make every effort to work through the problems, pains, and issues. Especially the big ones. The apostle Peter wrote, "Above all, keep fervent in your love for one another, because love covers a multitude of sins" (1 Pet 4:8). I believed his words when I first began in ministry, but I have come to appreciate their depth and value far more after 25 years. If God blesses me with another 25 years to live with and minister to family, I'm sure I'll treasure the truth of them even more.

I'm Not Afraid

This morning, I'm somewhere in the Caribbean, living out childhood dreams of being a pirate. The Scout Master and I have taken ten scouts to the Bahamas for a week of sailing. Neither the flight nor the sailing is unusually dangerous and so I expect to come home safely with adventurous stories and nothing worse than a mild sunburn. Still, accidents do happen. I've spoken at two funerals in the past few weeks. Others who were very close to me had their lives suddenly, tragically, and without warning, end. It is the end of every man, and the living do well to take it to heart (Eccl 7:2).

Before leaving, I wrote out a short will. There isn't too much to fuss over, but it's enough that I'm concerned inheriting it would not be a blessing to my children right now. So, I explained what I'd like for them to do if something were to happen to me. Besides that, and to me more importantly, I shared with them a few last heartfelt words about my faith. I've written them here in this article so they remain permanent. They cannot be forgotten after years, like the sound of a loved one's voice can. My children can reread them and know my last thoughts were of them, their souls' well-being, and my faith. You may find these words encouraging too.

—

I don't foresee anything bad happening. Lots of boys and leaders make this trip and are perfectly safe, but if something should happen to me in the air or out at sea, I don't want you to think that I was scared. If I don't come back to see and hug you, then I want you to know that I've gone to see Jesus. He has been my friend for a very long time. He has walked with me and even carried me through some heartbreaking and lonely seasons in life. He has also filled my life with wonderful joys. He is my constant friend. I have no reason to be afraid to see Him.

His Father and my Father will be waiting there to greet me, too. I expect God will welcome me just like I hug each of you when you come home. Wouldn't any good dad greet their son or daughter, who's been away for months or even years, this same way? And there is nothing to fear in going home to see your dad (1 Jn 4:17-18).

If something happens to me, I want you to know these things. Take comfort in them. I'm not gone; I've just moved. I've packed up my tent and campsite, and now I'm relaxing at home. You don't need to worry or be afraid for me. I want to give you that comfort. I also want you to think about something - if we traded places, could you give me that same comfort? Could you assure me that you know where you are going? Are you going to see a friend or are you a stranger to Jesus? Will you run up to hug your Father or will you dread meeting Him, ashamed and guilty of doing what He's told you not to do?

No matter what adventures you have in life, be sure you know the way home.

Love Pa

www.ingramcontent.com/pod-product-compliance
Lightning Source LLC
Chambersburg PA
CBHW042337040426
42447CB00017B/3465